F. G. COCKMAN

Discovering
Preserved
Railways

SHIRE PUBLICATIONS LTD

ACKNOWLEDGEMENTS

The cover photograph is by Wayne Finch. Other photographs are acknowledged as follows: P. Aldridge, page 24; D. W. Allan, Welsh Highland Railway (1964) Ltd, page 128; P. Briddon, page 8; P. E. B. Butler, page 54; F. G. Cockman, pages 13 (top), 36, 40, 47, 58, 65 (both), 69, 76, 82, 86, 96, 98, 101, 113, 123; Colne Valley Railway, page 31; J. J. Davis, pages 92, 106, 119; Brian Fisher, page 85; Commander R. Francis, page 125; Vaughan H. Gallois, page 18; Peter Groom, page 50; Peter Harris, page 27; Melvyn Hopwood, page 78; David Horne, page 13 (bottom); Isle of Wight Steam Railway, page 61; Cadbury Lamb, pages 4, 59, 142; Llanberis Lake Railway, page 72; Nene Valley Railway, page 81; North Yorkshire Moors Historical Railway Trust Ltd, page 91; C. A. Proctor, page 89; Keith Sanders, page 17; South Tynedale Railway, page 110; Steve Standbridge, page 45; Tony Stephens, page 28; D. Thom, page 117; Peter Thompson, page 134; West Somerset Railway, page 133; M. Willis, page 130; B. Woolner, page 23. Cartography is by Richard Holmes and Robert Dizon.

The publishers acknowledge with gratitude the assistance of Keith L. Lewis in the preparation of this fifth edition. They are also grateful for the invaluable help received from the managers of many of the railways in checking the accuracy of their entries.

Cover: Ex-GWR 2-8-0 no. 2857 on a freight train near Hailes Abbey bridge on the Gloucestershire Warwickshire Railway on 19th October 1992.

British Library Cataloguing in Publication Data: Cockman, F. G. (Frederick George), 1902-. Discovering Preserved Railways. – 5th ed. – (Discovering; 253). 1. Railroads – Great Britain – History. 2. Railroads – Great Britain – Timetables. 3. Railroads – Great Britain – Conservation and restoration. I. Title. 385'. 0941. ISBN 0-7478-0347-1.

NOTE

Locomotives and rolling stock are sometimes moved from one railway to another or taken out of service for long periods for repair. Therefore readers should be aware that some of those that are mentioned in the text will probably not be seen when they make a visit.

Published in 1997 by Shire Publications Ltd, Cromwell House, Church Street, Princes Risborough, Buckinghamshire HP27 9AA, UK.
Copyright © 1980 and 1995 by F. G. Cockman. First published 1980. Second edition 1985. Third edition 1990. Fourth edition 1995. Fifth edition 1997. Number 253 in the Discovering series. ISBN 0 7478 0347 1. F. G. Cockman is hereby identified as the author of this work in accordance with Section 77 of the Copyright, Designs and Patents Act 1988.

Printed in Great Britain by CIT Printing Services, Press Buildings, Merlins Bridge, Haverfordwest, Pembrokeshire SA61 1XF.

Contents

CONTENTS

Embsay & Bolton Abbey Steam Railway. Hunslet 0-6-0ST no. 68005 waiting to depart from Embsay station in June 1995. Note the Midland Railway type semaphore.

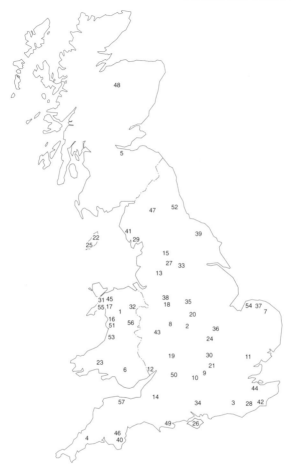

*Map of preserved railways. The numbers refer to the chapter numbers;
refer to Contents on pages 3-4.*

Preface

Railway preservation may be said to have started in Great Britain with the founding of the Talyllyn Railway Preservation Society in 1950, and it has since spread over the country from Bodmin to Aviemore. Other countries, like Germany, Holland, Belgium and France, have their preserved lines, but it is appropriate that Britain, where the railway was invented, should lead the way in the number so maintained. The founders of the new Talyllyn Railway might have been pardoned if they had paraphrased Pitt and said: 'The Talyllyn has saved herself by her exertions, and will, as we trust, save others by her example.' Apart from the miniature railways, the preserved lines could be divided into two kinds: those which had taken over private companies where failure was due to the exhaustion of the mineral deposits for which they were created; and those which wished to revive services on branches for which the British Transport Commission and later the British Railways Board had no further use.

The difficulties were daunting. For example, the Festiniog Railway had to see part of its track, including a tunnel, submerged by a new reservoir created by the Central Electricity Generating Board and had to construct an entirely new stretch of line with a new tunnel. In the case of the Kent & East Sussex Railway the necessary Light Railway Order was withheld year after year. Both of these railways ultimately triumphed, but only, as elsewhere, by means of enthusiasm, hard work and money. In defence of British Rail it must be stated that the effects of the Transport Acts of 1947, 1953 and 1962 were inevitably detrimental. Again, the abandonment of steam was necessary if the railways were to compete with modern motorway traffic and the airlines. Those who love the steam locomotive also admit that it caused air pollution, involved extremely dirty work in its maintenance and was thermally inefficient. Quite different considerations apply to the preserved railways, and we rely on them to show us the majesty of the steam locomotive, both in sight and in sound, and long may they continue to do so. Preservation provides an interesting, if challenging hobby to thousands of young people, many of whom may decide to make railways their career in life.

I have received much help from the press and publicity officers of various railways and this I record with great pleasure. Where photographs have been provided, due acknowledgement is given. Finally I wish to thank my old friend John Davis, MSc, CEng, MIMechE, for his unstinted help, not only with photographs, but also from his intimate knowledge of railway operation.

F. G. COCKMAN   *Bedford*

1. Bala Lake Railway

Headquarters. Yr Orsaf, Llanuwchllyn, Gwynedd LL23 7DD.
  Telephone: 01678 540666.
Origin. Bala & Dolgellau Railway: opened 1868, closed 1965.

After the closure of this important connection between Ruabon and mid Wales a group of enthusiasts was formed under the leadership of Mr G. H. Barnes, and a company was inaugurated in 1971 to revive the services as far as possible. Thus the Bala Lake Railway came into being, its name in Welsh being Rheilffordd Llyn Tegid. Instead of relaying a short length of standard-gauge track it was wisely decided to invest in a longer line with a gauge of 1 foot 11⅝ inches (600 mm) and the permanent way has been laid so well that the stock rides very smoothly. The distance from Llanuwchllyn to Bala Lake station is 4½ miles (7.2 km). The first train ran in 1972 and there is now a service from Easter to the end of September on a daily basis except certain Mondays and Fridays in the early and late season. Voluntary work is done by the Bala Lake Railway Society to help run the trains, the society's name in Welsh being Cymdeithas Rheilffordd Llyn Tegid.

Llanuwchllyn station buildings are the only original ones now standing of the former Bala & Dolgellau Railway, although the

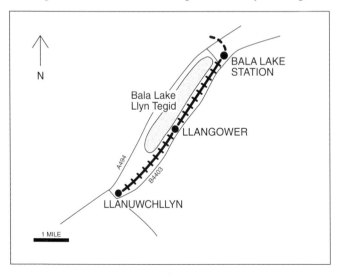

Bala Lake Railway. 0-4-0ST 'Maid Marian' (Hunslet 822/1900) at Llanuwchllyn station awaiting departure to Bala.

platform canopy was originally at Pwllheli in 1907, coming to Llanuwchllyn via Aberdovey in 1979. The station has a shop, refreshment room and stores. Here also are the locomotive repair shops. The signal box is the original GWR box and frame and is believed to be the only double-twist lever locking frame still in use. Visitors are welcome to inspect the box. The route runs alongside Bala Lake (Llyn Tegid) with pretty views, and it is not surprising that 20,000 passengers use the line each year.

There are two locomotives, powerful enough to cope with the 1 in 70 gradients, which regularly haul the trains. These are: *Maid Marian,* 0-4-0ST (Hunslet 822/1903); *Holy War* (Hunslet 779/1902). The railway also has a Bo-Bo diesel-hydraulic manufactured by Severn Lamb, reminiscent of a WR Hymek.

The railway conveys its passengers in comfortable bogie coaches dating from 1972 to 1982. This is a very friendly railway and a warm welcome is given to all visitors.

2. The Battlefield Line

Proprietors. Shackerstone Railway Society Ltd.
Headquarters. Shackerstone Station, Shackerstone, Leicestershire
   CV13 6NW. Telephone: 01827 880754.
Origin. Ashby & Nuneaton Joint Railway: opened 1873; closed to
   passengers 13th April 1931, closed to freight 1970.

The Ashby & Nuneaton Joint Railway was promoted by the London & North Western Railway and the Midland Railway. These joint ventures were typical of the latter half of the nineteenth century, by which time the principal cities and towns had railway connection. Further extension of the rail network involved expenditure which had to be justified by the probable financial return. Hence companies often preferred to share the expense and the profit arising. As will be judged from the closure dates, the chief revenue was from coal although it would appear that the L&NWR derived some benefit from passenger traffic. Just before the Grouping in 1923 the L&NWR ran seven passenger trains daily each way between Nuneaton and Loughborough (Derby Road) and to encourage traffic they opened halts with the attractive names of Thringstone, Grace Dieu and Snell's Nook. The Midland on the other hand contented themselves with one train each way between Nuneaton (Abbey) and Ashby de la Zouch. Obviously their main traffic was from the Leicestershire coalfields. Today the demand for coal has considerably diminished.

The Preservation Society was formed in 1969 and its objective was to reopen the 4^1/2 miles (7.2 km) of standard-gauge railway from Shackerstone to Shenton. After a great deal of effort a train service was commenced in 1978 as far as Market Bosworth, and by 1992 the present terminus of Shenton had been reached. Shackerstone station has been fully restored with entrance hall, booking office and Victorian tea rooms. Here also are a museum and a gift shop and the period atmosphere is maintained by advertisement signs, platform trolleys and the like. There is a pleasant picnic area near the Ashby Canal. The railway then passes through pretty countryside to the station of Market Bosworth, 2^1/2 miles (4 km) to the south. Here the station buildings have also been restored to their Victorian condition, and in addition there is a signal box to control the passing loop. 2 miles (3.2 km) further south is Shenton station, the buildings having been transferred from the former Midland Railway station of Humberstone Road by the laborious process of dismantling and re-erection. Humberstone Road station, just to the north of Leicester, was closed in 1968. Most visitors to

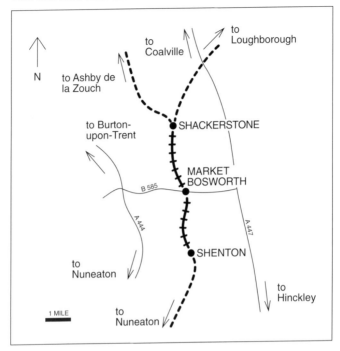

Shenton will take advantage of a visit to the Bosworth Battlefield Country Park, which is adjacent.

The motive power consists of a large number of industrial locomotives such as 0-6-0 *Lamport* no. 3, 0-4-0ST *Linda*, 0-4-0ST *Waleswood* (both undergoing restoration), and diesel locomotives which include no. 25265 *Harlech Castle*. Trains are mostly composed of former British Rail coaching stock and there is a large assortment of goods vehicles.

Train services are provided from Easter to the end of November. There are special events throughout the year, including a fortnightly Tudor Rose wine and dine service, and there are Santa trains in December.

3. Bluebell Railway

Headquarters. Sheffield Park station, Uckfield, East Sussex. Telephone: (general) 01825 723777; (talking timetable) 01825 722370.

Origin. Lewes & East Grinstead Railway (absorbed by London Brighton & South Coast Railway): opened 1882, closed 1955; reopened 1956, closed finally 1958.

One year after the final closure of the 'Bluebell Railway' there was great public support for the proposed Bluebell Railway Preservation Society, so that it was possible to run the first train from Sheffield Park to Horsted Keynes in 1960. The first closure in 1955 had contravened a clause in the original act to the effect that four trains daily should run over the line in perpetuity, and this provision had to be carried out by the British Transport Commission until they secured fresh legislation to relieve them, and the second closure then came about. At first the new Bluebell Railway was not allowed to use the Southern Region station at Horsted Keynes and constructed its own halt a little to the south. In due course the problem was resolved by the management of the new Bluebell purchasing the buildings and track outright.

Since then such progress has been made that train services operate daily from Easter to October, and there are Santa Specials at Christmas. Thus the Bluebell Railway was the first of the preserved lines of standard gauge in the passenger-carrying business. (The Middleton Railway, opened two months earlier, was concerned chiefly with freight.) At Sheffield Park station there is an excellent refreshment room, named the Bessemer Arms, and a museum. In the yard there are engine sheds and a well-equipped workshop for locomotive repairs.

At present the trains run from Sheffield Park to Horsted Keynes, thence through Sharpthorne Tunnel to West Hoathly, a distance of 8 miles (13 km), and Kingscote, 10 miles (16 km), through the pretty Sussex countryside. Work is now in progress on the final section to East Grinstead. At Horsted Keynes there are refreshment rooms and a bookshop and every endeavour is made to preserve a 'Brighton' appearance. There is ample parking space at each station and the visitor can move on to the famous Sheffield Park Gardens (National Trust) after a trip on the line. The Bluebell Railway carries 291,000 passengers annually.

The 'Bluebell' possesses a fine collection of steam locomotives, the most notable being: ex-SECR – three P class 0-6-0Ts nos. 27, 323 and 1178; H class 0-4-4T no. 263; C class 0-6-0 no. 592; ex-

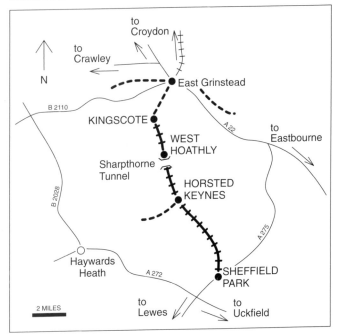

LBSCR – two 'Terrier' 0-6-0Ts nos. 55 and 72; E4 0-6-2T no. 473; ex-LSWR – 4-4-2T no. 488; 0-4-0T no. 96; ex-NLR – 0-6-0T no. 2650; ex-GWR – 4-4-0 no. 3217; ex-Southern Railway – 21C123 *Blackmore Vale*, U class 2-6-0 nos. 1618 and 31638; Q class 0-6-0 no. 30541; Q1 class 0-6-0 no. C1; 4-6-2 no. 34059 *Sir Archibald Sinclair*; USA 0-6-0T no. 30064; S class 4-6-0 no. 30847; British Rail locomotives – Standard class 2 2-6-0 no. 78059; class 4 4-6-0 no. 75027; class 5 4-6-0 no. 73082; 2-6-4T no. 80100; 2-10-0 no. 92240. Also, there is now a Fletcher Jennings 0-4-0T no. 158 (1877).

The gradient of 1 in 75 to Horsted Keynes thus presents no problems. At Horsted Keynes there are modern carriage sheds where maintenance can be carried out on such famous stock as the Metropolitan 'Ashbury' set, the SECR 'Birdcage' brake/third and the LNWR Blaenau branch observation coach. In addition to the LBSCR milk van there are several LSWR and Southern Railway coaches.

Bluebell Railway. GWR 'Dukedog' class 4-4-0 no. 3217 (formerly 9017) 'Earl of Berkeley' about to leave Sheffield Park for Horsted Keynes.

Bodmin & Wenford Railway. 0-6-0ST no. 62 'Ugly' at Bodmin Parkway, July 1990.

4. Bodmin & Wenford Railway

Headquarters. Bodmin General station, Bodmin, Cornwall. Telephone: 01208 73666.

Origin. Bodmin & Wadebridge Railway: opened 4th July 1834, closed 30th January 1967. Cornwall Railway: opened 4th May 1859, closed October 1983.

For a county town, Bodmin was unfortunate with its railway connections. It was very early in the field, having its first railway in 1834, but this ran only to Wadebridge and was isolated for many years. The Cornwall Railway was opened on 4th May 1859, the day following the Prince Consort's visit to Saltash to open Brunel's famous bridge over the Tamar, but this railway could provide a station only at Bodmin Road (now called Bodmin Parkway), $3^1/2$ miles (5.6 km) from the town. This was not very serious at that time but later the Great Western Railway, which had worked the Cornwall Railway since 1861, built a branch to Bodmin from Bodmin Road, and this was opened on 17th May 1887. The GWR absorbed the Cornwall Railway in 1889. The behaviour of the London & South Western Railway was strange, because, having bought the Bodmin & Wadebridge line in 1845, they did not open their station at Wadebridge until 1st June 1895. This was a railway which fell a victim to Beeching's 'Reshaping of British Railways' and was closed on 30th June 1967. It is to the Great Western's credit that they ran nine trains a day in each direction between Bodmin Road and Bodmin.

The closure by British Rail of Bodmin General station in October 1983 was followed in July 1984 by the formation of a Preservation Group, the members of which wished to reopen the line and thus create the only preserved railway of standard gauge in Cornwall. Such was the interest engendered that the members of the Bodmin & Wenford Railway were able to see their first train run in June 1990. Moreover, a new halt, named Colesloggett, was opened between Bodmin Parkway and Bodmin General stations.

The visitor to the railway will be amply rewarded. For example, before departing by train, he or she will be able to walk across to Lanhydrock garden, which is of great beauty, and, if time permits, to visit Restormel Castle. The train's first stop after Parkway is Colesloggett Halt, which is close to Cardinham Woods. Here are a cafe and facilities for cycle hire. The train then proceeds to Bodmin General station, where there is a buffet and a shop, and nearby are the Duke of Cornwall's Light Infantry Museum and Bodmin Museum. In 1996 the line was extended to Boscarne Junction, where a

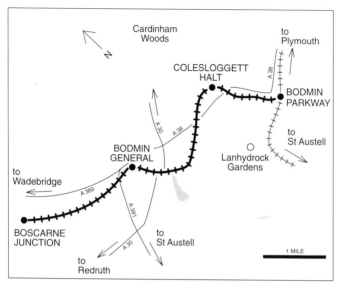

new station has been built. At this point a footpath and a cycle track run along the bed of the former Bodmin & Wadebridge Railway. Formerly, trains carrying Cornish clay ran from the pits at Wenfordbridge to Boscarne Junction, and there is a possibility that the Department of Transport will allow this line to reopen in order to divert lorry traffic from the country lanes.

The company has an interesting collection of locomotives. They are of the 0-6-0ST type – *Swiftsure* (Hunslet 2857/1943), *Ugly* (Robert Stephenson & Hawthorne 7673/1950) – with several diesels of classes 08, 10, 20, 31, 33, 50 and 108. Engines being restored for future use are GWR 2-6-2T nos. 4575 and 5552, 2-8-0 nos. 2884 and 3802 and Southern 4-6-2 no. 34007 *Wadebridge*.

Trains run from April to October and there are many events such as a 'Thomas the Tank Engine' weekend and at Christmas the usual Santa and Mince Pie Specials.

5. Bo'ness & Kinneil Railway
(The Scottish Railway Preservation Society)

Headquarters. The Station, Union Street, Bo'ness, West Lothian
EH51 9AQ. Telephone: 01506 822298 or 822446.

Origin. Part of the Slamannan Railway from Airdrie to Bo'ness:
extension from Slamannan to Bo'ness opened 17th March 1851.
Later link to Edinburgh & Glasgow Railway (Bo'ness Junction):
the station here was Manuel, which had high-level platforms on the
E&G and low-level below. The low-level line closed 1930. Lat-
terly passenger service was from Bo'ness to Polmont or Larbert.
This closed to passengers in 1955. From 1960 to 1981 the branch
served Kinneil pit, following the closure of Bo'ness dock and
related sidings between Kinneil and Carriden.

The Scottish Railway Preservation Society was formed in 1961
and always intended to display its collection operating on a branch
line, but for many years, while seeking a new home, it had a depot at
Falkirk (Springburn Yard). In 1979 work commenced on building a
line along the foreshore at Bo'ness from a point about half a mile
(800 metres) east of the original station, on a site devoid of all track
and buildings. A basic push-pull service first ran in 1981. Difficulties
in crossing pipelines to the BP works at Grangemouth meant that the
line had to follow a new alignment as it was extended to Kinneil,
where a platform was built complete with run-round loop. A train

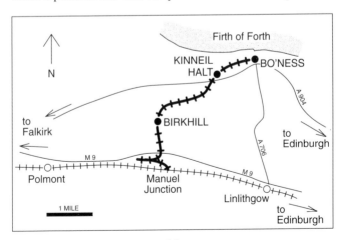

Bo'ness & Kinneil Railway. LMS Black 5 4-6-0 no. 44871 'Sovereign' entering Birkhill station.

service ran to Kinneil from 1984 to 1988. Meanwhile the transport of coal from Kinneil pit ceased in 1981, so making available the line to Bo'ness Junction. The SRPS could afford to buy only the lower 2 miles (3 km) and the other track was lifted and scrapped. Around this time the fireclay mine at Birkhill, which had not been rail connected for some years, also closed but was purchased by the Central Regional Council for the Bo'ness Heritage Trust. The aim was therefore to create a new station to give public access to this additional attraction. This work was completed in time to allow the railway to be extended to Birkhill in May 1989, giving a run of 3½ miles (5.6 km).

There remained another 1½ miles (2.4 km) to the former junction. This was relaid upon the closure of the Falkirk depot and a new connection made in the Edinburgh direction in 1989-90. This extension is not yet in public use but the connection is used regularly for the Society's railtour coaches to gain access to the network.

During this period buildings from various locations have been rebuilt on the railway. The station building at Bo'ness is from Wormit, along with the original Haymarket train shed of 1842. Monifieth station was given to the Society and moved to Birkhill in time for the opening in 1989.

Locomotives include North British Railway no. 653 *Maude* and an Austerity, no. 19. Many other locomotives are under active restoration and there is a pool of working ex-BR diesels.

In 1996 the Society opened a major display of rolling stock in a new building on the north side of the Bo'ness site. Known as the Scottish Railway Exhibition, this is open when the railway operates. The theme is largely the transport of freight but the display includes the two surviving NBR engines, *Glen Douglas* and the Y9 saddle tank.

Trains operate at weekends from Easter to the third weekend in October and daily, except Mondays, for six weeks from July to mid August. In December Santa trains operate, for which prior booking is required. Season tickets are available. For the latest leaflet send a stamped and addressed envelope.

Brecon Mountain Railway. 0-6-2WT 'Graf Schwerin-Lowitz' on a train returning to Pant station.

6. Brecon Mountain Railway

Headquarters. Pant station, Merthyr Tydfil, Mid Glamorgan CF48 2UP. Telephone: 01685 722988.
Origin. Brecon & Merthyr Tydfil Junction Railway: opened 1863, closed 1964.

After the closure of the line by British Rail a scheme was put forward to reopen the railway between Pant and Torpantau. This was in 1972 and the Brecon Mountain Railway Company was formed. The company was successful in obtaining a Light Railway Order and was further encouraged by the Brecon Beacons National Park Authority, which gave access to the park. The authority took the view that the railway would be able to convey visitors to the park with far less disturbance than would be caused by a large number of motorists entering the countryside. All vehicles were to be kept out of the park. Further assistance was forthcoming financially from the Wales Tourist Board, the Welsh Office and local authorities.

It was decided that the gauge of the new railway should be 1 foot 11¾ inches (603 mm) and an enormous amount of work confronted the company. A new station had to be constructed at Pant and a new alignment was therefore necessary. This involved the removal of 107,000 cubic feet (3000 cubic metres) of rock and the replacement of three bridges. There was vegetation to be removed from the trackbed, but the members of the company worked with great enthusiasm and the first train was able to run from Pant to Pontsticill in June 1980.

At Pant station the visitor will find a large car park, workshops, a licensed cafeteria, shop and toilets. Passengers in the train will first see on the left, and far below, the river Taf Fechan and then across the valley the village of Pontsticill. Then follows superb scenery with views of the Taf Fechan reservoir and the three peaks of the Brecon Beacons. The middle peak is Pen y Fan, which rises to a height of 2906 feet (872 metres), thus being the highest mountain in South Wales. After a journey of approximately 2 miles (3 km) the train arrives at Pontsticill and then proceeds to Dolygaer, 3½ miles (5.6 km), the present terminus. Passengers are not allowed to alight at Dolygaer. On the return journey, the train waits at Pontsticill, where passengers may alight for a short break. The ultimate aim of the company is to reach Torpantau station, which is 1300 feet (396 metres) above sea level. This will take the railway past the pretty Pentwyn reservoir and make a total length of railway of 5½ miles (8.9 km). The climb up to Torpantau will

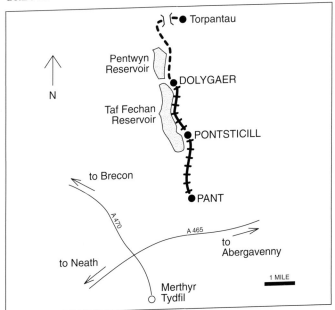

involve 1³/₄ miles (2.8 km) at a gradient of 1 in 47/49.

The company has an interesting collection of locomotives. These are: 0-6-2WT *Graf Schwerin-Lowitz*, built by Arn Jung, Germany, 1908; 0-6-0 diesel-hydraulic built by Brecon Mountain Railway, 1987; 4-6-2 with eight-wheel bogie tender, Baldwin Locomotive Works, 1930; 2-6-2+2-6-2 articulated tank engine, Hanomag, 1928 (this is the most powerful engine ever built for this gauge); 0-4-0VBT *Redstone*, built by Redstone of Penmaenmawr, 1905; 0-4-0WT by Orenstein & Koppel, 1936; 0-4-0VBT by De Winton, Caernarfon, 1894; 0-4-0ST by Hunslet Engineering Company, 1903.

The bogie coaching stock is very comfortable and was constructed by the company at their Pant workshops. There is an hourly train service from April to October.

7. Bure Valley Railway
The Broadland Line

Headquarters. Aylsham station, Norwich Road, Aylsham, Norfolk. Telephone: 01263 733858.

Origin. East Norfolk Railway: opened Wroxham to Buxton Lamas 8th July 1879, Buxton Lamas to Aylsham 1st January 1880; closed to passengers 15th September 1952, to goods 1982.

The main lines in East Anglia had been laid down between 1845 and 1847, so it is surprising to note that further railway expansion was taking place as late as 1880. The reason lay in the unceasing competition between the Great Eastern Railway and its smaller rivals, the Lynn & Fakenham Railway and the Yarmouth & North Norfolk Railway. When these two companies tried to amalgamate, the Great Eastern and its protégé the East Norfolk Railway successfully resisted the bill in Parliament in 1879. By contrast, the East Norfolk obtained its act for the 'Westward Extension' from Aylsham to Reepham, which was completed on 2nd May 1881. The GER absorbed the East Norfolk in 1882. In the meantime, the Lynn & Fakenham and the Yarmouth & North Norfolk Railways had joined with others to form the Eastern & Midlands Railway, which finally became the Midland & Great Northern Joint Railway in 1893. The GER and the M&GNJR then began a competitive war which was to last until nationalisation in 1948.

In the days before the Grouping (1st January 1923) the Great Eastern was running five trains per day each way between Aylsham and Wroxham but the patronage was never heavy. Passenger traffic declined rapidly after 1945 as a line of this rural type could not compete against the car and the lorry. But although passenger trains disappeared in 1952 British Rail continued to use the tracks for freight purposes until 1982. Fortunately the Broadland District Council acquired the trackbed for the purpose of making a public footpath between Aylsham and Wroxham, and this allowed sufficient space for the construction of a railway alongside. The Bure Valley Railway Ltd was then formed and in 1986 the construction of a 15 inch (381 mm) gauge railway, 9 miles (14.5 km) in length, was put in hand. The work involved a considerable degree of civil engineering skill. For example, a tunnel had to be bored under the A140 road, necessitating a gradient of 1 in 76 down from Aylsham, with a corresponding difficult climb for locomotives coming from Wroxham. A new station was opened at Brampton but the work was carried out so speedily that the first train ran in 1990.

East Anglia is far from flat and there is plenty of hard work for

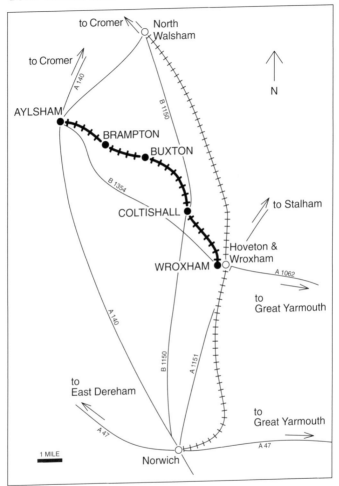

the locomotives over ten sections where the gradient is 1 in 100 or thereabouts. Near Brampton station there are delightful views of the river Bure. At Aylsham station the visitor will find a shop, tourist information centre and an inviting cafeteria. Here also are the railway workshops for the maintenance of rolling stock and locomotives. Train services are provided from Easter to the end of

Bure Valley Railway. 2-6-2 locomotive no. 6 with a train near Coltishall. Note the public footpath beside the line.

September and at Christmas. There are large free car parks at Aylsham and Wroxham.

The locomotives are of exceptional interest. No. 1 is a 2-6-4T named *Wroxham Broad*; there are two 2-6-2 (tender) engines based on the Indian Railways' ZB class. These are assisted by three diesel locomotives. There is a self-propelled, fully operational steam crane *Little Titan*, built in 1975 by E. Cheeseman. As the Bure Valley Railway has been built to the gauge of 15 inches (381 mm) the management is in the fortunate position of being able to exchange engines with the Ravenglass & Eskdale Railway and the Romney Hythe & Dymchurch Railway. These 'strangers' attract large numbers of the public. The BVR, with its situation in the Norfolk Broads, has a great potential.

The carriages have roofs and are equipped with comfortable seating. A further attraction is that all are air-braked, and electrically heated as occasion demands. The coach livery is red. There are five wagons for permanent-way maintenance. The railway operates two-day steam locomotive driving courses.

8. Chasewater Railway

Headquarters. Brownhills West station, Hednesford Road, Brownhills West, Walsall, West Midlands WS8 7LT. Telephone: 0121-355 3812 and 0121-359 2546; (timetable enquiries) 01543 452623.

Origin. Cannock Chase & Wolverhampton Railway, opened 1856, eventually passing into the hands of the National Coal Board, which ceased using the line in 1965.

The Chasewater Railway was re-formed in 1985 as a registered charity, to merge the assets of the earlier Railway Preservation Society (West Midlands) and the railway's operating company. Now operating as 'The Colliery Line' to reflect its origins and location in the heart of the Cannock Chase coalfield, the railway is situated in Chasewater Park, off the A5, Brownhills West, Walsall.

Although the focus is on industrial steam locomotives, the railway also operates heritage diesel locomotives on its passenger services, which run on Sundays and bank holiday Mondays from Easter to mid October. Santa Specials normally operate on the two Sundays immediately before Christmas.

A new station at Norton Lakeside, just across the causeway

Chasewater Light Railway. Hawthorne Leslie 0-4-0ST 'Asbestos' (1909) with a Millfield School special train.

between two lakes, was opened in December 1995, thus providing a round trip of about 2½ miles (4 km). The railway is already planning a further extension of another half mile or so.

Steam locomotives currently in use are: 0-4-0ST *Asbestos* (Hawthorn Leslie, 1909) and 0-4-0VBT *Sentinel* (Sentinel, 1957). Currently under restoration are 0-4-0ST *Alfred Paget* (Neilson, 1882) and 0-6-0T no. S100 (Hudswell Clarke, 1949). Also under restoration is L&Y petrol locomotive no.1 (Motor Rail, 1919), believed to be the first petrol locomotive on the capital list of any main line railway.

The railway has a number of interesting items of rolling stock, both passenger and goods, together with a wide range of steam and diesel locomotives either under restoration or 'awaiting their turn

9. Chinnor & Princes Risborough Railway
The Icknield Line

Headquarters. Chinnor railway station, Station Road, Chinnor, Oxfordshire. Telephone: 01844 354117 or 353535 (timetable).

Origin. Watlington & Princes Risborough Railway: opened 1872, closed to passengers 1957, to goods 1961; traffic to Chinnor cement works discontinued 1989.

Like so many small railways, the Watlington & Princes Risborough Railway had no rolling stock of its own, and it was worked by the Great Western Railway from the start. The larger line absorbed it in 1883. The line ran through pretty countryside, but at first there were stations only at Chinnor, Aston Rowant and Watlington. The stations at Chinnor and Aston Rowant were of attractive design, having central offices flanked by two pretty gable ends. The track was single and the distance between bridge buttresses showed that it was intended to remain single.

After 1900 the Great Western, in common with other leading companies, installed halts at various places where the villages were near the line. This attempt to stimulate passenger traffic was manifested by halts at Bledlow Bridge between Princes Risborough and Chinnor, Kingston Crossing between Chinnor and Aston Rowant, and Lewknor Bridge between Aston Rowant and Watlington. Later a halt known as Wainhill was opened near Chinnor. Shortly before the Grouping of 1923 the Great Western advertised that the service was maintained by 'Autocars', with one class only, on weekdays. There was no Sunday service. The branch had a service of five trains each way, the first leaving Watlington at 8.40 but the first from Princes Risborough was not until 10.02.

This was because there was only one engine in steam, shedded at Watlington. To its great credit, the Great Western arranged for a coach to be slipped at Princes Risborough from the express leaving Paddington at 9.10 (to connect with the 10.02 for Watlington), and another from the 19.10 Birmingham express (to connect with the 19.57 branch train). After 1945 the branch service was maintained by the ubiquitous GWR 0-6-0PTs.

A glance at a map shows that a branch line like this was vulnerable to road competition as only Chinnor station and Lewknor Bridge halt were near the villages they purported to serve. Watlington station was about 1 mile (1.6 km) from the town. The cessation of passenger trains in 1957 was six years before the Beeching report, 'The Reshaping of British Railways'. Even the goods traffic ceased before Beeching, but a cement works near Chinnor kept the northern part of the line open until 1989. Four months before the final closure the Chinnor & Princes Risborough Railway Association was formed and promptly arranged to purchase the line as soon as the last cement train ran. Rapid progress was made in restoring the pretty station at Chinnor, and a service of

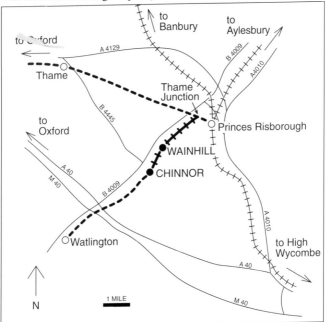

Chinnor & Princes Risborough Railway. Diesel locomotive no. D8568 approaching the newly constructed platform at Chinnor on 1st May 1994.

trains as far as Thame Junction began on 14th April 1995. At present, passengers cannot alight there and must make the round trip from Chinnor. The trains include a travelling bookshop and buffet car, and the service is six trains per day at every weekend from April to October. There are nine special events, which include Santa and Mince Pie specials for ten days in December. At present motive power is provided by ex-BR 0-6-0 diesel no. D3018, D8568 and 0-6-0ST *Sir Robert Peel*; additions will be made in due course. Passengers enjoy the comfort of former BR vestibuled stock. The ultimate aim of the C&PRR is to extend to Princes Risborough (4 miles; 6.4 km) and the volunteer workers are to be congratulated on what they have achieved so quickly. Further motive power has been acquired in the form of Ruston & Hornsby diesel *Iris* and ex-BR no. D08011 and a most useful addition is the Class 122 'Bubble Car' 55003. The C&PRR have been able to purchase the body of a Cambrian Railways' six-wheel third-class coach, no. 4106, which provides station facilities at Chinnor. There is a passenger stock in GWR chocolate and cream livery and a good selection of freight stock.

10. Cholsey & Wallingford Railway

Headquarters. St John's Road, Wallingford, Oxfordshire. Telephone: 01491 35067.

Origin. Cholsey & Wallingford Railway: opened 2nd July 1866, closed 15th June 1959.

The original intention of this company had been to join the Wycombe Railway, which had opened from Maidenhead to High Wycombe on 1st August 1854. For financial reasons this was not achieved and the branch carried on quietly until purchased by the Great Western Railway in 1872. The larger company had been unable to decide on a permanent name for the junction station, as it had opened as 'Moulsford Road' on 1st June 1840, a year before the main line was opened throughout to Bristol. Six months later the name was altered to 'Wallingford Road', and when the Cholsey & Wallingford line was opened the junction was renamed 'Moulsford Junction for the Wallingford Branch'. In 1892 the station settled down to its final name of 'Cholsey & Moulsford'. The branch was 2³/4 miles (4.4 km) long and in 1922 had a daily service of thirteen trains in each direction.

Efforts to reopen the branch were soon in evidence for as early

Cholsey & Wallingford Railway. Former Midland Railway 0-6-0T engine no. 41712, on loan from the 1708 Trust, Swanage, being unloaded at Wallingford on 27th August 1993.

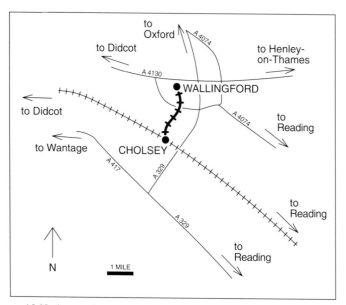

as 1968 short train rides were given to the public by means of 0-4-2T no. 1466, sent by the Great Western Society of Didcot. In 1969 British Rail saw fit to demolish Wallingford station buildings and the line remained open solely for traffic to a malt factory. This traffic ceased in 1981. Efforts by volunteers resulted in the creation of a new station building and platform and, furthermore, the track was restored to passenger train standards so rapidly that a Light Railway Order was granted after inspection in 1985. The new Cholsey & Wallingford Railway now possesses 2 miles (3 km) of track but trains had to stop short of Cholsey station (Railtrack). In future, however, they will be allowed to use the old bay in Cholsey station.

The railway is now open on Sundays and bank holidays from Easter to the end of September and there are special events such as Easter Bunny trains, Thomas the Tank Engine in August and the December Santa services.

The railway is accumulating an excellent collection of motive power and coaching stock, the most notable locomotive being the former Great Western Railway 2-8-0T no. 4247. To complete a realistic atmosphere, freight trains are run from time to time. Diesel power is represented by class 8 0-6-0 no. D3190. At the new Wallingford station visitors will find refreshments, a shop and a museum.

11. Colne Valley Railway

Headquarters. Castle Hedingham station, Yeldham Road, Castle Hedingham, Essex CO9 3DZ. Telephone: 01787 461174.
Origin. Colne Valley & Halstead Railway: opened 1863, closed 1962.

The first Colne Valley & Halstead Railway was a line of marked individuality and remained quite independent of its important neighbour, the Great Eastern Railway, pursuing its own course from 1863 until 1923, when it was merged into the London & North Eastern Railway. It ran from Chappel & Wakes Colne Junction to its own terminus at Haverhill, although later it used the GER station there. The CV&HR possessed an interesting collection of locomotives and rolling stock, although these were gradually replaced by LNER stock. The Beeching era was a dangerous one for the smaller railways and the CV&HR duly succumbed. Fortunately, local people were sufficiently interested to have trains running again in the Colne valley, and in 1973 they formed the Colne Valley Railway Company Ltd. They soon acquired locomotives and the main problem was to have their own stations and track.

By means of extraordinary enthusiasm and hard work the new company arranged for the complete dismantling of Castle Hedingham station and its re-erection on another site. This is on one platform of the new station, and on the other they have built an exact reproduction of Halstead station. Here there is the locomo-

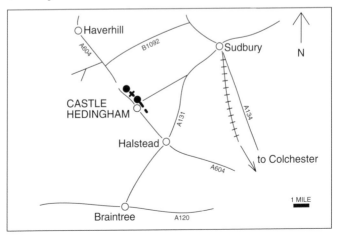

Colne Valley Railway. Castle Hedingham station, photographed soon after its re-erection, with Avonside 0-4-0ST no. 1875 'Barrington'.

tive yard and at present there is 1 mile (1.6 km) of track available for train services, with an extension to Halstead in the future giving another 4 miles (6 km). This is only the beginning.

There are regular services from March to October, and also Santa Specials. The company has a number of industrial locomotives, among them being: ex-WD 0-6-0ST no. 190, 0-4-0ST no. 1875, 0-6-0T no. 40 and 0-6-0ST no. 68072. There is a large collection of passenger and goods vehicles.

There is a 5 acre (2 hectare) woodland picnic area, buffet facilities are available on operational days, and a Pullman Sunday lunch is served on the train if pre-booked. Motorists using the A120, A131 and A134 roads should finally take the A604 which passes Castle Hedingham station.

12. Dean Forest Railway

Headquarters. Norchard, Forest Road, Lydney, Gloucestershire GL15 4ET. Telephone: 01594 845840 or for 'talking timetable' 01594 843423.

Origin. The Severn & Wye Railway (horse tramway), by Act of Parliament 1809. Freight operation continued until the late 1970s.

This interesting line was taken over jointly by the Great Western and Midland railways in 1923. The line lost its passenger service to Parkend, Coleford and Cinderford in 1929 but services continued to Lydney Town until shortly after the demise of the Severn Bridge in October 1960.

Local enthusiasts wishing to preserve the line formed the Dean Forest Railway Preservation Society in 1970, establishing a base at Parkend. British Rail, undecided about ending the dwindling freight traffic, refused to sell the Lydney to Parkend line to the DFRPS and the society moved to Norchard, the site of the old colliery and West Gloucestershire Power Station, in 1975. In 1980 British Rail decided to sell up and the line was purchased. The DFR had already committed itself to developing Norchard and operating southwards and thus no work was put into the line from Norchard to Parkend until recently. From Norchard to Lydney Junction (Severn & Wye) work progressed and the line was gradually reopened: St Mary's halt (formerly Lakeside) was reached in August 1991 and Lydney Junction reopened in 1996. Work has since commenced on the Parkend section of the line, which may reopen in 1998.

Norchard, the railway's base, has an excellent shop, a museum and other facilities including a cafeteria car open on all operating days. The railway's workshop and restoration shed is also here.

The railway is open for viewing every day with the shop and museum open Wednesdays, Saturdays and Sundays from January to March and every day from April to December. Timetabled steam services run on Sundays from April through to September, on Wednesdays in June, July and August, plus Thursdays and Saturdays during August. Special events include Thomas the Tank Engine during May bank holiday week and September, Santa Specials during December and Wilbert's New Year Party during New Year.

The railway is home to the following locomotives: ex-GWR 2-6-2Ts 5541 and 5521, ex-BR (W) 0-6-0PT 9681, ex-TVR no. 28 plus three Hunslet 0-6-0 tanks, a number of industrial diesels and a class 108 dmu.

13. East Lancashire Railway

Headquarters. Bolton Street station, Bury, Lancashire. Telephone: 0161-705 5111 and 0161-764 7790.
Origin. Manchester Bury & Rossendale Railway: opened 1846, closed 1966.

Soon after the first trains ran between Bury and Rawtenstall the company changed its name to the East Lancashire Railway. The year 1846 was the time of the Railway Mania, which resulted in the rapid development of the Lancashire railway network. For example, the important Manchester & Leeds Railway had also opened throughout in 1846 and almost immediately amalgamated with the Manchester & Bolton Railway. Then followed the absorption of ten other companies, including the East Lancashire Railway. Such a large combine required a different name, and thus the Lancashire & Yorkshire Railway came into being in 1847. There was now a rapid development, with Accrington being reached in 1848 and Bacup in 1852, the routes dividing at Stubbins Junction. The Lancashire & Yorkshire Railway became a system of great complexity and faithfully served this part of England until 1922, when it amalgamated with the London & North Western Railway.

The closure by British Rail of Bacup station on 5th December 1966 gave rise to the formation of the East Lancashire Railway Preservation Society in 1968 and they soon opened a museum at Bury with an excellent collection of locomotives and rolling stock. The closure of Rawtenstall station on 3rd June 1972 gave no scope for further development by the Society as freight trains continued to use the track until 4th December 1980. After the closure of a line British Rail always hastens to lift the track, and this often involves preservationists in considerable trouble and expense in restoration. The society had by now formed the East Lancashire Railway, who were most fortunate in enlisting the help of the local authority and the Department of the Environment. Prompt action from this source prevented track lifting and this saved the East Lancashire Railway much expense. Nevertheless a great deal of work had to be done by volunteers to bring the line up to passenger traffic standards, but this was accomplished and the necessary Light Railway Order was awarded in 1986.

The first train ran on 25th July 1987, since when a service of eight trains daily has been provided. A normal passenger service is maintained throughout the year, with the special days which have become normal on many preserved lines. On the ELR there is a Teddy Bear Picnic in August, Thomas the Tank Engine in

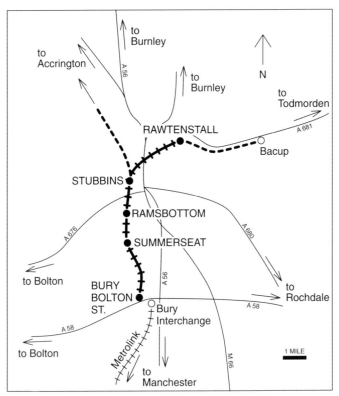

September, and at the Christmas period the public can enjoy the Santa Specials.

The railway has a praiseworthy collection of motive power. Included are Stanier class 5 4-6-0 no. 45337, former LMS 2-8-0 no. 48274, Ivatt class 2 2-6-0 no. 46428, Great Western 2-8-0T no. 4229, and British Rail Standard locomotives 2-10-0 no. 92207, 4-6-0 no. 73156, 2-6-0 no. 76079 and 2-6-4T no. 80097. Industrial engines are Hudswell Clarke 0-6-0T no. 680 (1903) and Hunslet 0-6-0ST no. 3789 (1953). Diesel power is represented by D832 *Onslaught*, D1041 *Western Prince*, class 40 nos. D335, D345 and 40145, class 24 no. D5054 and Hymek no. D7076. There are also some diesel shunting locomotives.

14. East Somerset Railway

Headquarters. Railway Station, Cranmore, Shepton Mallet, Somerset. Telephone: 0174 988457.

Origin. East Somerset Railway: opened 1858, closed 9th September 1963.

The East Somerset Railway was opened as part of the Great Western system in 1858 and extended for 31½ miles (50.7 km) from Yatton Junction through Cheddar, Wells and Shepton Mallet to Witham Junction. It thus joined the original Bristol & Exeter Railway of 1844 to the 'new' West of England main line of 1906. Although it was a popular holiday line its situation in sparsely populated country to the south-west of the Mendips meant that it would never be very profitable. Thus it became an early victim of the 'Reshaping of British Railways' plan of 1963. The Great Western Railway had never run more than five trains a day in each direction.

In 1974 the East Somerset Railway was formed by the well-

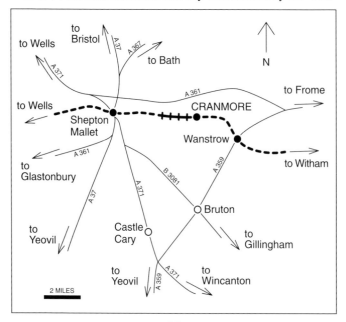

East Somerset Railway. The engine shed at Cranmore, built as an exact replica of Great Western style. In the foreground is SR 'Schools' class 4-4-0 no. 928 'Stowe'.

known artist David Shepherd, a lover of steam locomotives. Approximately 2 miles (3 km) of track have been cleared and brought up to the required standard. In consequence, a Light Railway Order was issued in 1978. Cranmore station deserves a visit on account of its having been fully restored in Great Western style; at the same time a new engine shed has been built to conform with Great Western design and locomotive workshops have been constructed. The East Somerset Railway is open from May to October and there is a special day at the end of August when Cranmore Village Fair is held. As on other railways, Santa trains are run at Christmas.

In view of David Shepherd's interest in steam locomotives it is not surprising to find an excellent collection at Cranmore. There are class 9 2-10-0 no. 92203 *Black Prince*, class 4 4-6-0 no. 75029 *Green Knight*, LMS type 0-6-0T no. 47493, GWR 0-6-2T no. 6634, 0-6-0ST no. 68005, former LBSCR E1 0-6-0T no. 110, and others, making a total of ten. For passenger trains there is an ample supply of bogie stock and also a large collection of goods vehicles.

15. Embsay & Bolton Abbey Steam Railway

Headquarters. Embsay station, Embsay, Skipton, North Yorkshire BD23 6AX. Telephone: 01756 794727; (talking timetable) 01756 795189.

Origin. Embsay to Grassington: opened 1902, closed to passengers 1930, to freight 1965.

The Embsay to Grassington line was a branch off the Skipton to Ilkley railway (opened 1888), and trains commenced running to Grassington in 1902. The private companies did not often close branches, but the London Midland & Scottish Railway withdrew the passenger service from Embsay to Grassington in 1930. Freight trains conveying limestone continued to run until 1968 and when it appeared that these trains would disappear owing to lessening output the Embsay & Grassington Railway Preservation Society was formed. On the Skipton-Ilkley branch the first casualties were stations like Bolton Abbey, which closed first in 1940 and re-opened in 1941. The second closure came in 1965 when the line proved to be yet another Beeching victim, and there was no preservation society to save it.

In 1969 the Preservation Society changed its name to the Yorkshire Dales Railway Society, and the first train ran in 1970. It was renamed the Embsay Steam Railway and in 1997 the Embsay & Bolton Abbey Steam Railway. Surprisingly the limestone quarries

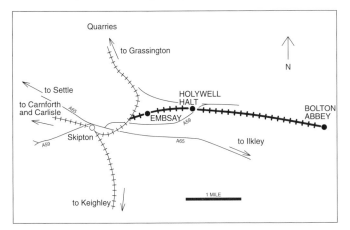

have increased their production so that they require the line for freight and the railway has extended along the route to Ilkley. Holywell halt became the terminus while Bolton Abbey station was being restored for the extension of the line there in summer 1997. Train services operate on Sundays, Tuesdays and Saturdays in July, with trains on Wednesdays during August. There are also special events such as Easter Egg Specials, Halloween Specials and the usual Santa Specials at Christmas.

Haulage is entrusted to industrial-type tank engines, notably Hunslet 0-6-0T no. 3715 (1951), bearing the name *Primrose* and numbered 2; another called *Wheldale*, no. 3168 (1944); an 0-4-0ST by Yates Duxbury, no. 1159 (1908) called *Annie*; and 0-6-0ST no. 7169 (1945). Coaching stock is LMS derived.

16. Fairbourne & Barmouth Steam Railway

Headquarters. Beach Road, Fairbourne, Gwynedd LL38 2PZ. Telephone: 01341 250362.
Origin. Opened in 1896 as a horse-drawn 2 foot (610 mm) gauge railway.

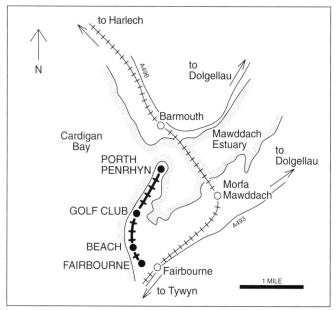

The English name 'Fairbourne' proclaims the village as being a late Victorian development as a seaside resort in Wales. The 2 mile (3.2 km) railway running from the village to the Mawddach was nearly derelict at the end of the war in 1945 but fortunately a company was formed to acquire the assets and relay the track to a gauge of 15 inches (381 mm). As the line was extended to reach the ferry it is very easy to go across to Barmouth. There is an intermediate stop called Golf Club Halt.

In May 1984 a new company took over. The gauge was altered to 12^1/4 inches (311 mm) for the 1986 season. In April 1995 a new company bought the assets. Services operate during Easter week, then weekends only until May. From May to mid September trains run daily. Locomotive stock includes 0-4-0ST *Sherpa,* 2-6-4T *Russell,* 2-6-2T *Yeo* and diesel 1A-A1 *Lilian Walter.*

17. Festiniog Railway

Headquarters. Porthmadog, Gwynedd. Telephone: 01766 512340.
Origin. Opened in 1836 for carrying quarried slate in horse-drawn wagons. Passenger conveyance began in 1865. This ceased in 1939 and freight in 1946.

Between 1807 and 1810 a causeway was built across the river Glaslyn near Porthmadog as part of a scheme to reclaim land. The embankment is known as the Traeth Mawr causeway but is usually referred to as 'The Cob'. This engineering work was to play a great part in the history of the railway. In 1832 James Spooner obtained an Act of Parliament for the construction of a line from Porthmadog

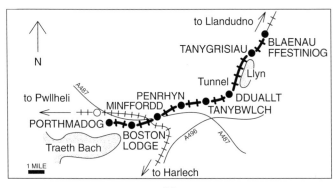

*Festiniog Railway. 0-4-4-0T 'Earl of Merioneth' (formerly 'Taliesin')
at Minffordd.*

to Blaenau Ffestiniog for carrying slate down to the coast for
export. He surveyed the route with such ability that he was able to
maintain an average gradient of 1 in 92, thus making it possible for
horses to haul the empty wagons up to Blaenau, while the loaded
ones ran gently down, controlled by brakesmen, with the horses
riding in a 'dandy car' at the rear of the train. This operation began
in 1836, only four years after work on the line commenced. When
James Spooner died in 1859 he was succeeded by his son, Charles
Spooner, who decided that the railway could be more efficiently
worked by steam. Although doubts were expressed on the feasibi-
lity of building a successful locomotive to such a small gauge as 1
foot 11^1/$_2$ inches (597 mm), George England & Company undertook the work and supplied four 0-4-0 engines, *The Prince, The
Princess, Mountaineer* and *Palmerston,* which commenced their
successful career in 1863, thus displacing the horses. They easily
hauled a train of 50 tons up to Blaenau Ffestiniog. Two years later
the Board of Trade gave permission for fare-paying passengers to
be carried. The stock was increased by two more locomotives of
similar design, named *Welsh Pony* and *Little Giant.* The Festiniog
made history with its next engine, also by George England, of 0-4-
4-0T design, named *Little Wonder.* This design of two powered
bogies enabled the engine to pull a train of nearly 200 tons up the

40

gradient. It is therefore not surprising that more similar locomotives followed: *Merddin Emrys*, built by the company in their works at Boston Lodge, and *Livingston Thompson*, also a home product. The latter has been renamed twice, firstly *Taliesin* and then *Earl of Merioneth*. Boston Lodge works has built Fairlie-type 0-4-4-0T *Earl of Merioneth* (1979) to replace the original of that name that now resides in the National Railway Museum and *David Lloyd George* (1993).

Passenger services ceased in 1939, and declining slate traffic brought complete closure of the line in 1946. As a result the 13 miles (21 km) of track soon became covered in vegetation, which grew worse in the nine years before the next train ran. The Festiniog Railway Society was formed in 1954 with the object of reopening the system, and a trust was created in 1964. The volunteers of the society worked to such effect that in 1955 trains ran from Porthmadog to Boston Lodge, and each year brought progress so that by 1968 the line was open to Dduallt. A misfortune had struck the railway in the meantime in that the Central Electricity Generating Board had obtained powers to build a dam and raise the water level to such a degree that Moelwyn Tunnel (between Dduallt and Tanygrisiau) was flooded. The response of the Festiniog Railway was to divert the track and to raise its level by means of a spiral, constructing a shorter tunnel. In 1979 the Gwynedd County Council agreed to the building of a new terminal site at Blaenau Ffestiniog for the use of British Rail and the Festiniog Railway. It was opened in May 1982. For the better accommodation of passengers there are now two platforms at Blaenau Ffestiniog, and coaching stock is now kept under cover at Glan-y-Pwll.

Today trains run at some weekends in the winter and daily from the end of March to early November. Santa Specials are run in December. The stations on the Festiniog are: Porthmadog, Boston Lodge, Minffordd, Penrhyn, Plas, Tanybwlch, Dduallt, Tanygrisiau, Blaenau Ffestiniog. Many trains have refreshment cars and, in view of the delightful scenery, it is not surprising that 440,000 passenger journeys are made annually. Porthmadog and other stations have refreshment facilities. The present locomotive stock in service includes 0-4-0STT *Prince* and *Palmerston,* 0-4-4-0T *Earl of Merioneth* and *David Lloyd George,* 2-4-0STT *Linda* and *Blanche* (ex-Penrhyn Quarry Railway), 2-6-2T *Mountaineer* (USA) and numerous diesel locomotives. Trackside safety is ensured by having most locomotives converted from coal to oil burning. There is also an interesting collection of coaching stock, including many original coaches still in use, some from 1865.

The Festiniog is the oldest narrow-gauge passenger-carrying railway in the world.

18. Foxfield Steam Railway

Headquarters. Caverswall Road station, Blythe Bridge, Stoke-on-Trent, Staffordshire ST11 9EA. Telephone: 01782 396210 and 01270 874959.

Origin. Colliery railway running from Blythe Bridge (North Staffordshire Railway) to Foxfield Colliery: closed 1965.

The Foxfield Railway Society was formed as soon as the collieries were closed, with the object of running a service of passenger trains for pleasure purposes over $3^1/2$ miles (5.6 km) of track from Foxfield Colliery to Blythe Bridge (Caverswall Road). A vast amount of work has been carried out to improve the track (although steep gradients remain) by members of the Society, and at the same time they have been able to collect an interesting assortment of locomotives and rolling stock. There is a workshop for maintaining engines and coaching stock in good working order. An excellent railway museum has been opened at Caverswall Road.

Trains run from Easter to September with the usual family attractions such as Friends of Thomas the Tank Engine in May and August, and in July and August freight trains are run specially to interest visitors. In 1993 special trains were run to mark the centenary of the railway. The section from Dilhorne Park to Foxfield Colliery has been reopened for goods trains and in due course will

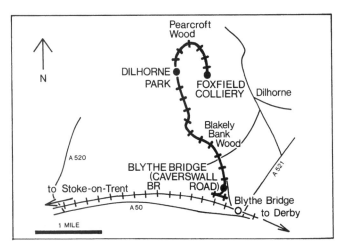

be passed for passenger traffic. There is an interesting assortment of passenger and goods vehicles and the locomotive stock comprises: Bagnall 0-6-0ST *Lewisham* (1924) and 0-4-0ST *Hawarden* (1940); Peckett 0-4-0ST *Henry Cort* (1903), 0-4-0ST *Ironbridge* (1933), *Lion* (1914) and no. 11 (1947); Hunslet 0-6-0ST *Whiston* (1950) and *Wimblebury* (1956); Robert Stephenson & Hawthorne 0-4-0ST *Roker* (1939) and crane engine no. 7006 (1940); Barclay 0-4-0ST *CPC* (1929); Kerr Stuart 0-4-0ST *Moss Bay* (1920); Avonside 0-6-0ST *Cranford* (1919); and also six diesel locomotives.

19. Gloucestershire Warwickshire Railway

Headquarters. The Railway Station, Toddington, Gloucestershire. Telephone: 01242 621405.

Origin. Great Western Railway, Birmingham to Bristol direct railway: opened 1st July 1908; closed to passengers 7th March 1960, entirely 1977.

Although the Great Western Railway had opened a route from Birmingham to Cheltenham via Banbury and Kingham on 1st June 1881 they desired a shorter connection and constructed a line via Stratford-upon-Avon and Honeybourne. The first train ran on 1st July 1908. This railway was intensively used by the GWR, there being, in addition to freight traffic, eleven trains each way daily between Honeybourne and Cheltenham. One of these was the famous 'Cornishman', which left Wolverhampton at 10.35 and arrived at Penzance at 19.55. In the other direction the departure time from Penzance was 10.30, the train arriving at Wolverhampton at 19.50. After 1948 there was the familiar story of declining traffic and economies effected by British Rail in diverting trains to nearby London Midland tracks. With complete closure of the direct line imminent, a group of enthusiasts was formed in 1976 to create a preservation society. In spite of this British Rail dismantled the entire route in 1979. However, such was the spirit of the Gloucestershire Warwickshire Railway supporters that rolling stock was obtained and track relaid, with the result that the first train ran on 22nd April 1984, marked by a ceremony in which Mr Nicholas Ridley, Secretary of State for Transport, cut the ribbon.

The line at present runs from Toddington to Far Stanley, a distance of 5¼ miles (8.5 km). Just after leaving Winchcombe station the train negotiates Greet Tunnel, which at 693 yards (634 metres) is the longest tunnel on a preserved railway. Near a former halt is to be found a thirteenth-century Cistercian abbey maintained by the National Trust. With a view to future expansion the railway has purchased the trackbed from Broadway to Pittville, a suburb of Cheltenham, a distance of 13 miles (21 km). In addition it has the option of purchasing the 4 miles (6.4 km) of trackbed between Broadway and Honeybourne. Although the trackbed north of Honeybourne belongs to several owners, purchase may one day be possible, so that trains may once again connect Stratford with Cheltenham. The entire district is one of enchanting scenery. Platforms have been rebuilt at Toddington and Winchcombe. The goods shed at the former station is now occupied as a locomotive repair shop, and at the latter station a similar building is used for the maintenance of coaching stock.

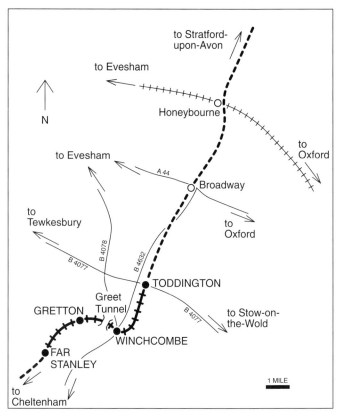

Gloucestershire Warwickshire Railway. GWR 2-8-0 no. 2857 at the head of a special honeymoon train near the summit at Winchcombe.

Trains run at each weekend from March to October, and during the summer season there are also weekday services. At Christmas there are Santa Specials, and in January Mince Pie Specials.

The railway possesses a number of industrial locomotives such as Peckett *John* (1976/1939), Hunslet *King George* (2309/1942), Robert Nelson no. 1800 (1936) and Bagnall *Byfield No. 2* (2655/1942). Several large locomotives are being restored, such as Great Western 2-8-0 no. 2807, 2-8-0T no. 4277 and no. 4936 *Kinlet Hall*. The stud will in due course be increased by Southern 4-6-2 no. 35006 *Peninsular & Orient SN Co*, and BR Standard 2-6-0 no. 76077. There are several others earmarked for the future such as GWR no. 7821 *Ditcheat Manor*, no. 5952 *Cogan Hall* and 2-6-2T no. 5526. There are some interesting diesel engines including class 47 no. 105. Coaching stock consists of eight BR Mark 1 vehicles, an ex-LMS inspection saloon and two Great Western coaches.

At Toddington the GWR have a narrow-gauge railway called the North Gloucestershire Railway, having a gauge of 2 feet (610 mm). The locomotives are: Jung 0-4-0WT *Justine*, Henschel 0-8-0T *Brigadelok* and Bagnall 4-4-0T *Isibutu*.

20. Great Central Railway

Headquarters. Loughborough Central station, Loughborough, Leicestershire. Telephone: 01509 230726.

Origin. The Great Central Railway opened its main line from Annesley to Quainton Road and Marylebone in 1899. It was closed in 1966 except for the section Rugby to Nottingham, which lasted until 1969. A suburban service is today maintained between Marylebone and Aylesbury.

The Great Central Railway was extended to London as 'the last main line' by the efforts of Sir Edward Watkin, who was chairman of the Manchester Sheffield & Lincolnshire Railway and also of the Metropolitan Railway. The running powers granted by the Metropolitan from Quainton Road to Harrow saved the Manchester Sheffield & Lincolnshire a considerable expense. The MS&LR changed its title to Great Central in 1897. The new line aroused mixed feelings. Passengers enjoyed a fast and reliable service under the guidance of the general manager, Sam Fay (later Sir Sam), and railway enthusiasts were delighted by the beauty of J. G. Robinson's locomotives. The ordinary shareholders were more sparing in their praise. The bills of 1892 (unsuccessful) and of 1893 (which became law) were bitterly opposed by the London & North Western and the Midland. The heirs in law of those two railways, namely the London Midland Region of British Rail, got hold of the GCR in 1966 and made short work of it.

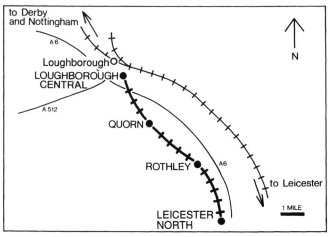

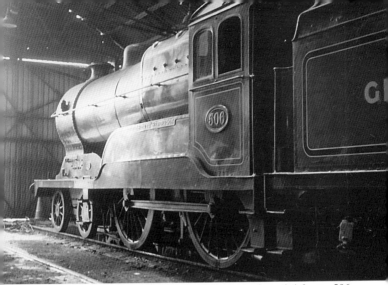

Great Central Railway. Robinson 'Director' class 4-4-0 no. 506 'Butler Henderson' on shed at Loughborough, 23rd May 1990.

It is not surprising that support for the revival of such a famous main line should be forthcoming and the Main Line Steam Trust was founded for this purpose. The trust was succeeded by the Great Central Railway Company (1976) Ltd for the purpose of instituting a service of trains on the former main line. The first train over the 5 mile (8 km) length ran in 1977. Trains run at weekends and on Wednesdays from May to September, but some include a restaurant car, in which an excellent four-course meal is served. The old GCR was laid with a ruling gradient of 1 in 176 so that the locomotives have an easy task.

The stations are: Loughborough, where there is a refreshment room and a site of 3¹/4 acres (1.5 hectares) of land on which are situated well-equipped repair shops; Quorn; Rothley; and Leicester North. There are plans to extend northwards to Ruddington when circumstances permit.

There is a splendid collection of locomotives, which includes the following: Collett GWR 2-8-0T no. 5224; LMS 4-6-0 no. 5231 (Black 5), which has been named *Third Volunteer Battalion Worcester and Sherwood Foresters Regiment*; LNER N2 0-6-2T in lined black; and former GCR 4-4-0 no. 506, on loan from the National Railway Museum. There are also BR Standard class 9 2-10-0 no. 92212 and D40-106. Southern 4-6-2 34101 *Hartland* and GWR 4-6-0 no. 6990 *Witherslack Hall* have been fully restored. SR no. 34039 *Boscastle* and ER B1 no. 1264 are in course of restoration, the latter being the property of the Thompson B1 Locomotive Society. More recent arrivals are LMR 2-8-0 no. 48305 and diesel no. 9529.

The new GCR has obtained two LNER buffet cars, which are used in the Thomas, Teddy Bear and Santa Specials.

21. Great Whipsnade Railway

Headquarters. Whipsnade Wild Animal Park, Dunstable, Bedfordshire LU6 2LF. Telephone: 01582 872171.

This is a new railway, dating from 1970, the purpose of which is to take visitors through the reserves containing wild animals, so that a close view with perfect safety can be obtained. Most of the animals come from Asia, such as elephants, yaks, camels, wild horses and many varieties of deer and antelope. The trains start and finish at Whipsnade Central station and thus run on a closed circuit of about 2 miles (3.2 km). The gauge is 2 feet 6 inches (762 mm). The hilly nature of the Dunstable Downs, which form part of the Chiltern Hills, has necessitated the building of embankments and the digging of cuttings and a tunnel. The railway operates at weekends in February, October and December and daily from March to September.

The locomotive collection is of interest as it includes two 0-6-0Ts named *Superior* (Kerr Stuart) and *Chevallier* (Manning Wardle). There is also a Kerr Stuart 0-4-2T *Excelsior*. Three diesel locomotives have stand-by duties. The railway also has a 1936 Smith & Rodley 5^1/$_2$ ton standard-gauge crane, and among the rolling stock are nine former Bowater Paper Mill wagons.

22. Groudle Glen Railway

Headquarters. Correspondence to: 29 Hawarden Avenue, Douglas, Isle of Man IM1 4BP. Telephone: 01624 670453 or 622138.
Origin. Groudle Glen Railway: opened 23rd May 1896, closed 1962.

When the Manx Electric Railway was opened in 1893 the number of visitors to Groudle increased enormously in view of the attractive scenery. As a further inducement it was decided to construct a dam across a rocky inlet and polar bears and sea lions were introduced for the edification of visitors. Three years after the arrival of the Manx Electric Railway a narrow-gauge line was opened from Lhen Coan to convey tourists to Sea Lion Rocks. The gauge was 2 feet (610 mm). Services were maintained by a locomotive named *Sea Lion* and three coaches, and Groudle Glen proved to be so popular that another engine named *Polar Bear* and additional stock had to be provided. The scenery of the glen was thus enjoyed by thousands of visitors for eighteen years, but the outbreak of war in 1914 caused the line to be closed. After 1919 the service recommenced but the steam locomotives were replaced by battery locos. These, however, were worn out after only six years' service but it was found possible to recondition the steam engines,

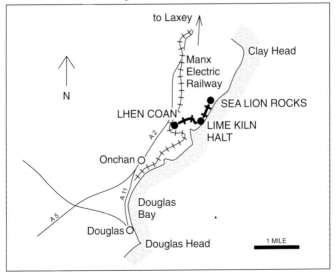

Groudle Glen Railway. 'Sea Lion' climbing the gradient towards Lime Kiln halt.

which continued to haul the trains until 1939. The Second World War caused a cessation of services until 1950, when the locomotive *Polar Bear* alone, with six coaches, served the public.

In addition to the fact that *Sea Lion* was not available for work, the company lost the use of the track between Headland and Sea Lion Rocks because of a landslip and in any event the zoo was closed and the animals were not replaced. The engine *Polar Bear* continued to work until 1962, but in the following year it needed heavy repairs. The closure in 1963 was followed by the disposal of the locomotives and coaches in 1967, and the removal of the track and demolition of buildings in 1973. It therefore demanded considerable resolution on the part of the members of the Isle of Man Steam Railway Supporters' Association to restore the Groudle Glen Railway in 1982, when work on clearing the site commenced. In addition, replacement track was obtained and after many months of hard work it was possible to reopen a section of the railway for passenger traffic in May 1986. What is even more encouraging is the restoration of the engine *Sea Lion* to working order by instructors and apprentices of BNFL Training College, Sellafield, and it has been at the head of trains since October 1987. After the clearance of the landslip the full length of the line from Lhen Coan to Sea Lion Rocks was opened in 1992. The public is therefore once more able to enjoy riding on this excellent railway.

Although the animals have long since departed from the pool at Sea Lion Rocks, the locomotive *Polar Bear* has also been restored and is now to be seen at Amberley Chalk Pits Museum, West Sussex. *Polar Bear* visited the line in 1993 and again for the railway's centenary in 1996.

The approach to the station is through the picturesque Groudle Glen, which is reached from Groudle Hotel. Trains run at Easter and on Sundays from May to September and on the normal bank holiday Mondays between 11 a.m. and 4.30 p.m. An attractive service is provided on Wednesday evenings between 7 p.m. and 9 p.m. in July and August. In December there are Santa trains and on Boxing Day Mince Pie trains. In addition to *Sea Lion,* the railway has two diesel locomotives, *Dolphin* and *Walrus,* 4 WDM, built in 1952 by Hudson Hunslet.

23. Gwili Railway
Rheilffordd Gwili

Headquarters. 49 Gabalfa Road, Sketty, Swansea. Telephone:
01792 201107. Information: Bronwydd Arms station, near
Carmarthen SA33 6HT. Telephone: 01267 230666.

Origin. Carmarthen & Cardigan Railway: opened 1st March 1860,
closed 1973.

The Carmarthen & Cardigan Railway was opened in 1860 but
failed to reach its objective, ending at Llandyssul. As it was
connected to the Great Western Railway it was built to the broad
gauge of 7 feet 0¼ inch (2140 mm). However, its traffic increased
after the opening of the Manchester & Milford Railway from
Pencader to Aberystwyth on 1st January 1866. The Great Western
worked the Carmarthen & Cardigan Railway from the commence-
ment and converted the track to the standard 4 feet 8½ inches
(1435 mm) from May 1872, when the whole of the South Wales
system was narrowed. The GWR absorbed the railway on 22nd
August 1881. In this quiet part of the Welsh countryside traffic was
never heavy and the passenger train service never exceeded five
trains each way per day.

British Rail closed the line in 1973 and the Gwili Railway

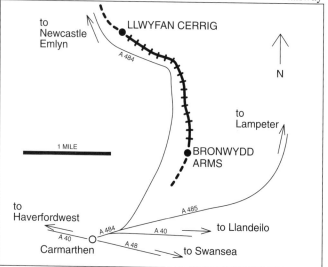

Gwili Railway. Barclay 0-4-0ST 'Rosyth no. 1' at the head of a train for Bronwydd Arms.

Company Ltd was formed in 1975 to purchase whatever track remained *in situ*, and, where it had been lifted, the trackbed was acquired. After the usual reclamation work was finished the necessary Light Railway Order was obtained, and trains began to run in 1978. The Gwili Railway has the distinction of being the first standard-gauge preserved line to reopen in Wales. The railway extends for about 2 miles (3 km) through very attractive countryside from Bronwydd Arms station to Llwyfan Cerrig. The route lies close to the pretty river Gwili. Train services are at Easter, Sundays in May, Spring Bank Holiday week, Wednesdays and Sundays from June to July, then daily from the last week in July to the end of August. Sunday only trains reappear in September, and there are trains in October, plus Santa specials.

The company has some interesting engines, such as a Robert Stephenson & Hawthorn 0-4-0ST and Hunslet 'Austerity' 0-6-0ST. The Vale of Neath Railway Society is now based at Gwili Railway, and its locomotive stock awaits restoration. The Gwili Railway has valuable items such as a Taff Vale Railway coach dating from 1891 and fully restored, and a signal box removed from Llandybie on the Central Wales line.

Bronwydd Arms station provides the usual facilities of large car park, refreshment coach (which used to run on the Cambridge Buffet Expresses), shop and toilets. At Llwyfan Cerrig there is a picnic site and a miniature railway. There is no road access. As the company owns several miles of trackbed it might be possible in the future to see trains running from Abergwili to Llanpumpsaint. Capital is now being raised to enable the railway to extend to Conwil Elfed, making a total length of over 3 miles (5 km).

24. Irchester Narrow Gauge Railway Museum

Headquarters. Irchester Country Park, Wellingborough, North-amptonshire. Telephone: 01604 675368.
Origin. Northamptonshire Locomotive Group, formed 1977.

For well over one hundred years the extraction of iron ore from the soil of Northamptonshire has been one of the county's principal industries. For example, the Stratford-on-Avon & Midland Junction Railway was opened in 1871 for the purpose of conveying iron ore to South Wales. Inevitably the ironstone deposits were being exhausted but more serious was the decline in the steel industry. In March 1981 Stewarts & Lloyds steelworks at Corby ceased production, after which there was the risk of the complete disappearance of the industry and its railways. It was therefore fortunate that the Northamptonshire Locomotive Group was able to purchase the Peckett 0-6-0ST no. 85 from Stewarts & Lloyds in 1985. In this year also the Irchester Narrow Gauge Railway Trust was formed as an educational charity, which administers the museum.

Irchester Narrow Gauge Railway Museum. On the day of the formal opening of the museum, 18th June 1988, the Mayor of Wellingborough stands beside Peckett 0-6-0ST no. 85.

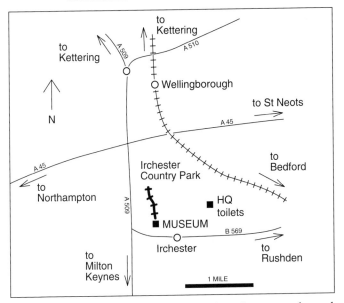

The locomotive and other industrial railway items were housed in the goods shed at Irchester station, which had been closed by British Rail to passenger traffic on 7th March 1960. When BR refused to sell the goods shed to the Trust it was felt that a removal to a more suitable site was essential for future development. Fortunately the local authority and the County Council were co-operative and the whole collection was removed to Irchester Country Park in 1987. Since then a great deal of work has been done by laying down track and erecting an engine shed and workshop. In 1990 the museum acquired another Peckett 0-6-0ST, no. 86, and it has since acquired a third, no. 87 (1942). There is now a representative collection of metre-gauge railway equipment. In order to be thoroughly comprehensive, the museum has acquired rolling stock for gauges of 1 foot 8 inches (508 mm), 2 feet (610 mm) and 3 feet (914 mm) with the requisite track. A very interesting acquisition is a Corpet 0-6-0T locomotive, *Cambrai*, dating from 1888, which is being restored in the workshops. There are several diesel engines for the 3 foot (914 mm) gauge track.

The site is open to the public on bank holidays and the last Sunday in each month from Easter to October. The museum, however, is open on every Sunday.

25. Isle of Man Railways

Headquarters. Strathallan Crescent, Douglas, Isle of Man IM2 4NR. Telephone: 01624 663366.

Origin. Isle of Man Railway: opened Douglas to Peel 1873, Douglas to Port Erin 1874; closed 1965.

In 1870 a company was incorporated for the purpose of developing railways in the Isle of Man. A gauge of 3 feet (914 mm) was decided upon and the 13½ miles (22 km) to Port Erin opened in 1874. The company throve and in 1904 took over the Manx Northern Railway, which ran from St John's up the west coast to Ramsey. At the height of its prosperity the Isle of Man Railway owned sixteen locomotives, 115 coaching vehicles and 175 goods vans and wagons. After 1945 a decline set in, as it did on the mainland, through road traffic, and despite satisfactory receipts from passenger traffic during the holiday period the company found that it could not make sufficient profit to make good its worn-out equipment. So closure came in 1965.

The past history of the Isle of Man Railway is exceedingly complex and the following paragraphs are intended to furnish the reader with a condensed account without sacrificing accuracy. As far back as 1928 the railway company had purchased its bus competitors to avoid wasteful rivalry, and services were maintained from that time, all through the Second World War, until the worn-out condition of the equipment and the flood of private cars on the island brought things to a head. If we take 1939 as being a peak period for the railway, then it is interesting to note that there were eight trains each day between Douglas and Ramsey via St John's both up and down, and nine between Douglas and Port Erin.

There came a day, however, when the management had to decide whether the revenue justified the vast expense of track renewals and locomotive repairs. The 1965 closure naturally brought protests from all railway lovers, so that by 1967 the sections from Douglas to Peel and Douglas to Castletown were reopened. In 1968 the trains were running again as far as Port Erin but a second decision to close was made. It was then that the Isle of Man Victorian Steam Railway Company Ltd was formed with plans to reopen the lines to Peel and Port Erin in the following year. The Isle of Man government promised to assist financially up to the sum of £7500. Some services were maintained in 1969 and 1970 but once more the financial result was disappointing. It would appear that the attempt to run services to both Peel and Port Erin had been too ambitious, so that in 1972 trains ran only between

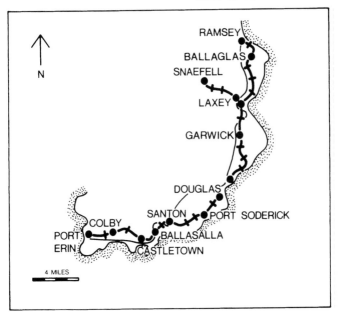

Douglas and Port Erin. It was in this year that Her Majesty the Queen visited the railway.

By 1975 the railway was showing a slight profit, although receiving £20,000 aid from the Manx government. The decision was made to sell the station buildings and site at Douglas, as they were very valuable, and to realise the scrap value of the rails lifted from the Ramsey line. The train services were reduced to the journey between Port Erin and Castletown (5¹/₂ miles or 8.9 km only) and the trains did not call at the two intermediate stations. Although the distance was increased in 1976 to the 8¹/₂ miles (13.7 km) between Port Erin and Ballasalla, the important development next year was the decision by Tynwald to nationalise the Isle of Man Railway by outright purchase. (It had already acquired the Manx Electric Railway in 1957.) The price was £250,000. As from 1st January 1978 the system has been known as the Isle of Man Railways, the steam division being the Isle of Man Railway, and the electric division the Manx Electric Railway.

Trains run from early April until the end of October, and the passenger figures are very satisfactory.

On the steam division the stations are Douglas, Port Soderick, Santon, Ballasalla, Castletown, Colby, Port St Mary and Port Erin.

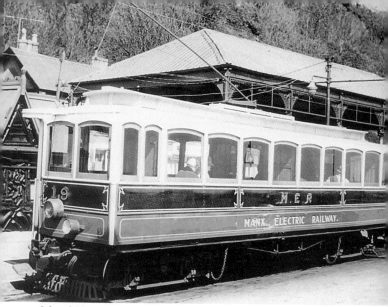

Isle of Man Railways. Manx Electric Railway power car no. 19 at Douglas.

The locomotives are mostly Beyer Peacock's 2-4-0Ts, and today they are: no. 10 *G. H. Wood*, no. 11 *Maitland* and no. 12 *Hutchinson*. Dubs 0-6-0T no. 15 *Caledonia* has been restored to working order and no. 17 *Viking* is a Schoema 0-4-0 diesel. The locomotives are kept very clean and look very smart in their green livery. All coaches are mounted on bogies; most have electric light.

The Manx Electric Railway was opened between Douglas and Ramsey, up the east coast, in 1893. The distance is 18 miles (29 km). The trains serve several places, the most important being Garwick, Laxey and Ballaglas. The cars collect current by means of trolley poles. At Laxey is also the station of the Snaefell Mountain Railway, having a gauge of 3 feet 6 inches (1067 mm). It was opened in 1895 and is 5 miles (8 km) long. Current is obtained through bow collectors and there is additional rheostatic braking. The Snaefell Mountain Railway has been equipped with a third rail reducing the gauge to 3 feet (914 mm) to enable the steam locomotive no. 15 *Caledonia* to reach the summit.

It must be gratifying to railway enthusiasts in the island, particularly to those who founded the Isle of Man Steam Railway Supporters Association, to find their railways at last on a firm foundation. The three lines not only provide public transport for the inhabitants but do much to add to the enjoyment of visitors on holiday. They can now enjoy the fascination of a steam trip to the south-west, ride on the electrics along the east coast and finally travel to the summit of Snaefell and delight, on a fine day, in the views of the sea and distant mainland.

Visitors to the island will also wish to ride on the Groudle Glen Railway, 2 miles (3 km) north of Douglas (see page 49).

Isle of Man Railways. Beyer Peacock 2-4-0T no. 10 'G. H. Wood' with a three-coach train on the Port Erin service in July 1994.

26. Isle of Wight Steam Railway

Headquarters. The Railway Station, Havenstreet, Isle of Wight
PO33 4DS. Telephone: 01983 882204; (talking timetable) 01983
884343.
Origin. Ryde & Newport Railway (Isle of Wight Central Railway):
opened 1875, closed 1966.

The railways of the Isle of Wight were always of great interest as
they were completely different from those on the mainland, so that
the visitor had the feeling of being in a foreign country. The first
railway on the island, between Cowes and Newport, was opened in
1862. This was followed by the Isle of Wight Railway, which
began running its trains between Ryde and Shanklin in 1864 and
on to Ventnor in 1866. The next development was the Ryde &
Newport Railway, opened in 1875, and its importance lies in the
fact that part of it is now preserved under the name of the Isle of
Wight Steam Railway. It had stations at Ashey, Havenstreet,
Wootton and Whippingham. In due course the island became well

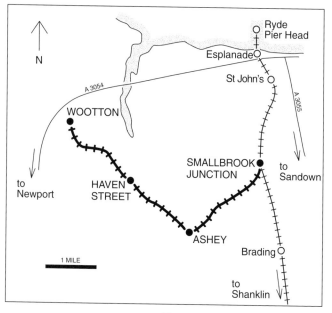

Isle of Wight Steam Railway. 'Terrier' 0-6-0T with a train of compartment stock at the new Wootton station.

supplied with railways. For example, the Isle of Wight (Newport Junction) Railway was opened in 1880 from Sandown to Newport, and a short branch from Brading to Bembridge in 1882. In 1887 the Cowes & Newport, the Ryde & Newport and the Isle of Wight (Newport Junction) amalgamated to form the Isle of Wight Central Railway. The west of the island was served by the Freshwater Yarmouth & Newport Railway, which began its operations in 1889, and the whole network was completed in 1900 when the IOWCR built its branch from Merstone to Ventnor (West).

By the provisions of the Railways Act (1921) all the island's railways were taken over by the Southern Railway, which spent a great deal of money in improving track, rolling stock and motive power. After nationalisation (1st January 1948) the Southern Region maintained services with an excellent stud of the attractive Adams O2 0-4-4T locomotives, which bore names and were always kept in their pristine condition. The livery was lined black.

In 1922, when most people travelled by train, the Isle of Wight Central Railway had provided Wootton and Havenstreet with eleven trains per day each way, but in course of time more and more cars arrived on the ferries. In consequence British Rail began their policy of retreat, the St Lawrence and Ventnor West line closing on 15th September 1952, the Freshwater Railway on 21st

September 1953 and Sandown to Newport on 6th February 1956. These dates are pre-Beeching (1963). The remainder (except Ryde to Shanklin) ceased in 1966. But even before closure a band of enthusiasts formed themselves into the Isle of Wight Locomotive Society and thus were able to purchase locomotives and rolling stock. One engine was no. 24 *Calbourne*. The vehicles were kept at Newport, but such was the impatience of British Rail to lift the track that a complete removal was made to Havenstreet on 24th January 1971. The newly formed Isle of Wight Steam Railway was therefore able to invite the public to Havenstreet in 1971.

Inevitably there was much to do before a Light Railway Order was obtained in respect of the track purchased between Havenstreet and Wootton. In addition to the usual clearing away of weeds and bushes, a new station had to be built at Wootton and at Havenstreet buildings had to be restored, signals erected and the signal box fully equipped. The LRO was granted in 1978, after the usual inspection by the Department of Transport. Trains began running immediately and since that time there has been a steady expansion. At Havenstreet station the visitor will find a refreshment room, a shop and a museum. The railway reached Smallbrook Junction in 1991, which is also served by electric trains running between Ryde and Shanklin. BR replaced the old rolling stock from the Piccadilly Tube used on this line with other rolling stock from London Transport.

The locomotive stock has an island flavour. For example, there is former London Brighton & South Coast Railway 'Terrier' 0-6-0T no. 8 *Freshwater*, and a similar engine, 32640 *Newport*, in black livery. As previously referred to, there is Adams 0-4-4T no. 24 *Calbourne* and also Hawthorne Leslie 0-4-0ST no. 37 *Invincible*. A more recent acquisition is 0-6-0ST no. 198 *Royal Engineer*. The steam engines are supplemented by two diesels, D2059 and D2554. The coaching stock is unique to preservation circles in consisting of wooden panelled compartment vehicles.

Train services are provided from April to October with several trains a day in the summer season. This railway has made remarkable progress since 1978.

27. Keighley & Worth Valley Railway

Headquarters. Haworth station, Keighley, West Yorkshire. Telephone: 01535 645214; (information service) 01535 647777.
Origin. Keighley & Worth Valley Railway (Midland Railway): opened 1867, closed 1962.

What might have been an obscure branch of the Midland Railway, closed by BR in 1962 and forgotten, has, by virtue of preservation, become one of the most famous in Britain. Keighley had been served by two railways, for in addition to the Midland, the Great Northern had opened a branch from their Leeds, Bradford and Halifax line, but this was closed in 1955. The Keighley & Worth Valley Railway Preservation Society had come into being soon after the Oxenhope branch was closed, but six years of hard work had to be done before the railway was ready for opening by virtue of a Light Railway Order. The first train over the 5 mile (8 km) branch therefore appeared in 1968.

Trains run each weekend all the year round, and daily from June to September. This is one of the railways which run Santa Specials at Christmas. The stations on the line are Keighley, which has refreshment rooms and forms a junction with BR, Ingrow, Damems, Oakworth, Haworth and Oxenhope. Haworth is the headquarters of the railway and has a large yard with running sheds and well-

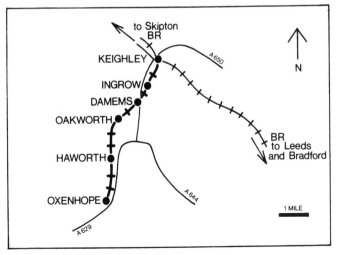

equipped repair workshops. Here there is a bookshop. Oxenhope station is the terminus and one can obtain refreshments there also, and in the yard are the new carriage sheds and a museum. At Ingrow station there is now an interesting collection of pre-Grouping passenger vehicles, with a new museum housing the Bahamas Loco Society and the Vintage Carriage Trust collections.

A journey on the K&WVR is of great interest. The gradients of 1 in 75 and even 1 in 64 give the locomotives plenty of hard work, with very satisfying sounds for the enthusiast. The industrial neighbourhood of Keighley is left behind and there are lovely views of the Worth valley. The hilly nature of the terrain has necessitated the boring of two tunnels, Ingrow and the longer Mytholmes. The annual number of passengers is 147,000 and they are attracted not only by the line itself but by the great number of locomotives to be seen in the yards at Haworth, Ingrow and Oxenhope.

The collection of locomotives includes: LYR 0-6-0 no. 957, two LYR 'Pugs' (0-4-0Ts), Midland 4F no. 3924, 0-6-0T no. 47279, GWR 0-6-0PT 57xx class no. L89, LMS 2-6-2T no. 41241, SR no. 34092 *City of Wells*, Swedish State Railway 2-8-0 (Riddles Austerity design), USA 0-6-0T no. 72, US/Polish 2-8-0 no. Tr203474, BR class 4 4-6-0 no. 75078, BR Standard class 2 2-6-0 no. 78022 (now fitted with a Giesl ejector) and 2-6-4T no. 80002, former LMS 2-8-0 no. 48431 and 2-6-0 no. 42765, LMR Black 5 no. 45212, Robert Stephenson & Hawthorne crane engine 7069/1941, Hudswell Clarke diesel 0-6-0 *Merlin* and a large number of industrial 0-6-0Ts and 0-4-0Ts, the latest being Peckett no. 1999 of 1941, and also two BR railbuses, nos. E79962 and M79964.

The coaching stock is varied and of great interest as it includes the NER directors' saloon, which appeared in the film *The Railway Children*. The vehicles are kept in capacious sheds at Oxenhope, while at Haworth there is a new locomotive shed. The film referred to, *The Railway Children*, was the second film of this story, the first having been made on the Southern Region's Horsham-Guildford branch. The Worth Valley film is the more famous, and it included splendid sequences of two locomotives at work; one was the LYR 0-6-0 no. 957, its black livery changed to bright green for the occasion, and the GWR/LTB 0-6-0PT no. L89. Oakworth station featured prominently in the film.

Visitors to this well-run line will derive great pleasure from it.

Keighley & Worth Valley Railway. Ivatt 2-6-2T no. 41241 at Haworth. This locomotive, very smart in its K&WVR livery and coat of arms, is ideal for the passenger service between Keighley and Oxenhope.

Keighley & Worth Valley Railway. Former Great Western Railway 0-6-0PT (London Transport no. L89) at Haworth.

28. Kent & East Sussex Railway

Headquarters. Tenterden station, Tenterden, Kent. Telephone: 01580 765155.
Origin. Rother Valley Light Railway: opened 1900, closed 1954.

The Kent & East Sussex Railway is always associated with the name of Lieutenant Colonel Holman Fred Stephens, whose activities in the sphere of light railways have become a legend. Although he died in 1931 he is well remembered and it is fitting that engine no. 23 of the K&ESR should be named after him. He was engineer and general manager to eight light railways: the East Kent, the Kent & East Sussex, the Weston Clevedon & Portishead, the Shropshire & Montgomeryshire, the Rye & Camber, the Festiniog, the Hundred of Manhood & Selsey, and the Snailbeach District. Of these his favourite was the Kent & East Sussex Railway.

The new Kent & East Sussex Railway was formed in 1962 and, although a satisfactory quantity of rolling stock was accumulated, the promoters had exceptional difficulty in obtaining consent from the authorities to commence working a train service. It was only through patience and determination of the highest calibre that they eventually succeeded. Time and again the Light Railway Order was withheld owing to objections by road users and planners, based partly on the number of level crossings *en route*. The Minister of Transport of that time was unsympathetic, but eventually

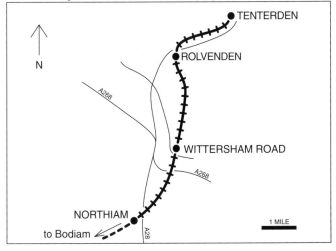

persistence was rewarded and trains began to move in 1974. The countryside in this part of Britain is unspoilt and attractive. Trains run at weekends from Easter to October and daily from the end of July to early September. At the weekends in summer there are delightful 'Wine and Dine' trains, with a special one named the 'Wealden Pullman'. At Christmas there are the usual Santa Specials. In view of these attractions the railway conveys fifty thousand passengers a year.

The stations include: Tenterden, with refreshment rooms, and sidings full of coaching stock undergoing restoration; Rolvenden, which has a yard full of locomotives and repair shops; and Wittersham Road, an attractive station completely renewed. The line has been extended to Northiam and future plans include an extension to Robertsbridge.

The locomotive stock includes: Hunslet 'Austerity' 0-6-0ST no. 23 *Holman F. Stephens* and no. 24; former LBSCR 'Terrier' nos. 3 *Bodiam* and 10 *Sutton*; Hunslet 204 horsepower six-coupled diesel no. 4708 of 1938; 0-6-0ST no. 14 *Charwelton* (Manning Wardle 1955/1917). Other 0-6-0T engines are two former SECR P class and two USA 'switchers'. Perhaps the most interesting is the locomotive from the Norwegian State Railway of 2-6-0 type. The recent acquisition of a 'Hastings' type diesel-electric multiple-unit set (nos. 60000, 60529 and 60016) will facilitate the maintenance of train services.

29. Lakeside & Haverthwaite Railway

Headquarters. Haverthwaite station, Ulverston, Cumbria. Telephone: 01539 531594.

Origin. Lakeside–Plumpton branch of the Furness Railway: opened 1869, closed 1965.

The Lakeside & Haverthwaite Railway Company was formed in 1970 and the 3 mile (4.8 km) stretch was opened in 1973. The first train ran only after much hard work in clearing the track and restoring it to passenger operating standards. Locomotives and stock had to be transported to Haverthwaite and the company is fortunate in possessing the two Fairburn engines.

Trains run from Easter to November and in December there are Santa Specials. The journey is through pretty scenery alongside the river Leven, and the terminus is situated at the south end of Lake Windermere. The stations are: Lakeside, Newby Bridge, and Haverthwaite.

Among the collection of locomotives may be seen: 0-4-0ST *Askham Hall* (Avonside no. 1772/1917); *David* and *Alexandra* (Barclay nos. 2333/1953 and 929/1902); Bagnall 0-6-0T no. 2682 *Princess*; GWR 0-6-2T no. 5643; and finally the two excellent ex-LMS Fairburn 2-6-4Ts nos. 2073 and 2085.

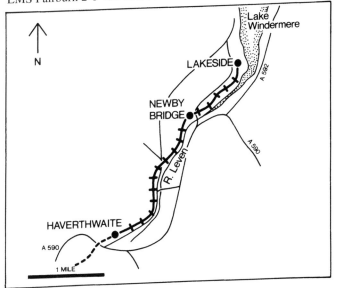

30. Leighton Buzzard Railway

Headquarters. Page's Park station, Billington Road, Leighton Buzzard, Bedfordshire LU7 8TN. Telephone: 01525 373888.
Origin. Industrial railway for sand excavation: opened 1919.

The First World War cut off sand supplies from Belgium and it became necessary to rely on sources from within Britain. The increase in demand led in 1919 to the construction of a narrow-gauge railway to link quarries and factories near Leighton Buzzard with a main line railhead. By 1969 road haulage had taken over the bulk of the sand traffic but some internal traffic continued until 1982. Meanwhile, in 1967, a group of enthusiasts had formed the Leighton Buzzard Narrow Gauge Railway Society and they ran their first train in 1968. This was an excellent performance and prevented the clogging of the line by vegetation, as has happened so often elsewhere. The state of the track, although good enough for sand wagons, was substandard for passenger work. Over the years, volunteers have completely rebuilt a 3 mile (5 km) stretch of the line, installing signalling, new rail, stations and facilities.

Leighton Buzzard Railway. Steam raising on 0-4-0ST 'Pixie' (Kerr Stuart, 1922).

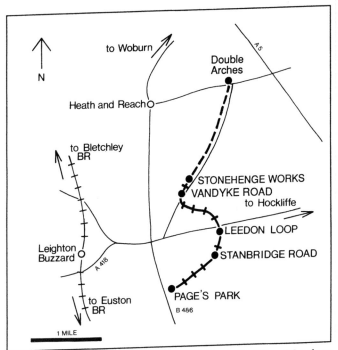

Train services run on Sundays and Bank Holiday Mondays from mid March to mid October, Wednesdays from June to August, and Thursdays and Saturdays in August, also at weekends prior to Christmas. The stations are: Page's Park, Stanbridge Road, Leedon Loop, Vandyke Road, and Stonehenge Works.

The railway possesses a real treasure in its locomotive *Chaloner*, an old vertical-boilered engine in working order. Other locomotives are 0-4-0ST no. 2 *Pixie*, 0-4-0T no. 3 *Rishra*, 0-6-0T no. 4 *Doll*, 0-6-0WT no. 5 *Elf*, 0-4-0WT no. 11 *P. C. Allen*, 0-4-0ST *Alice*, 0-4-0ST *Peter Pan*, and some diesel engines. There is some typical narrow-gauge coaching stock.

Page's Park station is signposted in and around Leighton Buzzard.

31. Llanberis Lake Railway
Padarn Lake Railway or Rheilffordd Llyn Padarn

Headquarters. Llanberis, Caernarfon, Gwynedd LL55 4TY. Telephone: 01286 870549.
Origin. Allt Ddu to Port Dinorwic, 1824.

The development of the slate quarries at Dinorwic required the construction of a railway, and in 1824 a track was laid down to be worked partly by gravity and partly by horses. As the trade grew this line was found to be inadequate and in 1843 the Padarn Railway was built to a gauge of 4 feet (1219 mm). It was worked by steam locomotives and the slate trade throve to such a degree that as many as 3000 workers lived in or near Llanberis. Two 0-4-0 locomotives for this railway were built at Northfleet in Kent and one was broken up in due course. The other, named *Fire Queen*, was left in its engine shed, which, when the doors became unserviceable, was sealed up with masonry. The locomotive lay forgotten until 1974, when it was cosmetically restored and put on display at Penrhyn Castle, Bangor, Gwynedd. This is a remarkable example

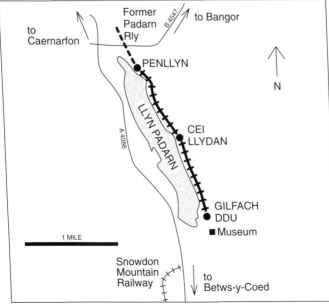

Llanberis Lake Railway. Hunslet 0-4-0ST locomotive no. 2 'Thomas Bach' at the head of a train near Llanberis Lake.

of early locomotive construction. Unfortunately the slate trade declined and the quarry was closed in October 1961. The track was lifted in 1969.

On the formation of the Llanberis Lake Railway in 1970 work was commenced on clearing the vegetation which had covered the trackbed in a short time. By July 1971 a new track of 1 foot 11½ inches (597 mm) gauge had been laid to Cei Llydan, and to Penllyn in 1972. The visitor will find a very large car park adjacent to the terminus station known as Gilfach Ddu, with toilet facilities. The station has a refreshment room and shop. The train is made up of comfortable coaches made in the railway's workshops. Most of the coaches are glazed, but the few open ones are attractive in hot weather. The journey is at first in a rock cutting but soon the train emerges and passengers obtain views of the Padarn Lake, one of the most beautiful in Wales.

The coaches have doors on the landward side only, as doors on the lake side of the vehicles might be dangerous for passengers. Trains wait at the intermediate station of Cei Llydan as there is a crossing loop here for traffic purposes. Train services extend from March to October.

There are four operating locomotives, which are well maintained by the company's workshops. They are no. 1 *Elidir* (named after the mountain), no. 2 *Thomas Bach* and no. 3 *Dolbadarn*. These are all steam 0-4-0ST engines made by Hunslet. The fourth, which is diesel-powered, is no. 8 *Twll Coed*. Visitors can spend a pleasant day in the picnic area adjoining Cei Llydan station, where there is also a woodland display centre and a children's adventure playground.

32. Llangollen Railway

Headquarters. The Station, Abbey Road, Llangollen, Denbighshire LL20 8SN. Telephone: 01978 860979 and (talking timetable) 01978 860951.

Origin. Ruabon–Llangollen–Corwen–Bala: railway opened between 1865 and 1868, by the Great Western Railway to standard gauge; closed 1965.

The Flint and Deeside Railway Preservation Society was formed in 1972. It subsequently became the Llangollen Railway Society in 1976, one year after occupying Llangollen station. The railway first started passenger services in 1981 over half a mile (800 metres) of track. It was permitted to operate as a steam centre pending its Light Railway Order being granted, which it obtained in April 1984. The line has since been extended through Deeside halt and Glyndyfrdwy to Carrog, and it is intended to continue to Corwen, 10 miles (16 km) from Llangollen.

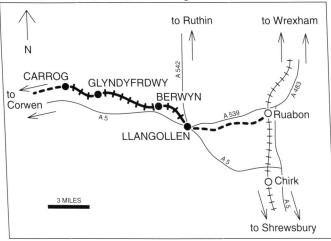

Train services are operated at weekends from January to March and in November, and daily from April through October. On Saturdays and Sundays during the season there is the 'Berwyn Belle' restaurant car service. Other attractions are Thomas the Tank Engine in June and September, and at Christmas there are Santa Specials, followed by Mince Pie Specials in January. Llangollen station is now restored to its Great Western aspect and has refreshment facilities and a shop. The original signal box is on platform 1. The Society is fortunate in having a line in a district of outstanding natural beauty by the valley of the river Dee. The town of Llangollen attracts large numbers of visitors for the International Musical Eisteddfod and there are the historic buildings of Dinas Bran Castle and Plas Newydd to be seen.

The locomotive stock naturally includes items of GWR interest such as 4-6-0 no. 7822 *Foxcote Manor* and no. 4936 *Kinlet Hall*. The LMS is represented by 0-6-0T no. 47298 and there are several industrial locomotives from Kitson, Fowler and Hudswell Clarke. Like most preserved railways, the Llangollen has acquired a number of diesel locomotives to attract visitors. These are class 25 nos. 7629 and 25313, class 24 no. 24081 and class 46 no. 46010. The rolling stock is mainly of GWR origin and there are workshop facilities for maintenance purposes.

33. Middleton Railway

Headquarters. Moor Road, Leeds LS10 2QJ. Telephone: 01532 710320.

Origin. The first Middleton Railway was laid in 1755 to a gauge of 4 feet 1 inch (1245 mm) to serve a colliery. The line was relaid and modernised in 1881. Closed 1958.

The Middleton Railway Trust was formed in 1958 soon after the colliery line ceased to operate, and by opening in June 1960 it had the distinction of being the first of the standard-gauge preserved railways. The railway operates between Moor Road and Middleton Park stations, a distance of $1^1/4$ miles (2 km). Trains run every Saturday and Sunday from Easter to October. A large new workshop with inspection pits has been constructed. This is known as the Fred Youell Building.

The Trust owns ten steam and seven diesel locomotives, including a Danish 0-4-0T (1895), an LNER Y7 0-4-0T, Manning Wardle 0-6-0ST *Arthur* (1601/1903), Sentinel 0-4-0VBT no. 68153, Hudswell Clarke 0-4-0ST *Mirvale*, and others from Peckett, Bagnall and Hunslet.

34. Mid-Hants Railway

Headquarters. Alresford station, Alresford, Hampshire SO24 9JG.
   Telephone: 01962 733810.
Origin. Mid-Hants Railway: opened 1865, absorbed by London &
   South Western Railway 1884, closed 1973.

Bradshaw's *Railway Manual* for 1869 states that the company
was incorporated in 1861 and was to be worked by the LSWR. The
length was 18¹/₂ miles (30 km), but unfortunately by 1869 the
company and its creditors had to appear before the Court of
Chancery. However, the LSWR continued to work the line and
eventually took it over completely. The chief product of market
gardeners in the district was watercress, and there was enough of
such traffic for the railway to be known as the 'Watercress Line'.
The proximity of the rivers Itchen and Alre encouraged the industry. Another claim to fame was that at Itchen Abbas station the
young Sam Fay started his railway career by being booking clerk
and general factotum. His subsequent career as general manager
first of the Midland & South Western Junction Railway and then of
the Great Central, culminating in a knighthood, is well-known. He
died in 1953 aged ninety-six and was buried in the churchyard at
Awbridge, not so very far from Itchen Abbas.
   The new railway company was formed soon after the closure and
volunteers worked to such good effect that the first train ran in

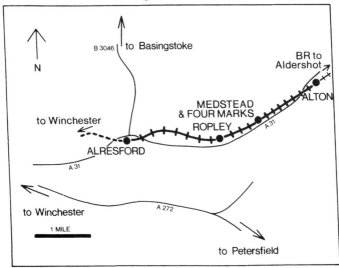

Mid-Hants Railway. BR Standard class 4 2-6-0 no. 76017 entering Medstead & Four Marks station with the 14.34 train to Alton on 14th June 1989.

1977. Train services are maintained over the 10 mile (16 km) line on most weekends from February to November with selected midweek running during June and daily running during all of July and August. In December the popular 'Santa Special' trains are run. The stations served on the line are Alresford, Ropley, Medstead & Four Marks and Alton. Footbridges have been newly erected at Alresford and Medstead & Four Marks.

There is an excellent collection of Southern Railway locomotives, including: N Class 2-6-0 no. 31874; U Class 2-6-0s 31625 and 31806; S15 4-6-0s 30506 and 30499; Bulleid 'Merchant Navy' Class nos. 35009 *Shaw Savill,* 35018 *British India Line* and 35005 *Canadian Pacific;* 'West Country' 4-6-2 34016 *Bodmin,* 34067 *Tangmere,* 34073 *249 Squadron* and 34105 *Swanage.*

Other locomotives include BR Standard class 5 4-6-0 no. 73096, BR Standard class 4 2-6-0 76017, a Baldwin 2-8-0 (70340/1944), an ex-LMS Ivatt 2-6-2 tank engine, no. 41312, and several Hunslet industrial 0-6-0Ts (one of which is permanently operated as 'Thomas the Tank Engine'). There are also three diesel locomotives, nos. 5353, 45132 and 08288.

The railway runs two dining trains: 'The Watercress Belle' and 'The Countryman'.

35. Midland Railway Centre

Headquarters. Butterley Station, Ripley, Derbyshire DE5 3QZ.
  Telephone: 01773 747674 or 749788; (visitors' information)
  01773 570140.

Origin. Ambergate station 11th May 1840; Trent to Pinxton 6th
  September 1847; Ambergate to Rowsley, 4th June 1849. Closures: Ripley 1st June 1930, Butterley 16th June 1947 to passengers.

It will be noticed that the Midland Railway system opened very
early in the history of railways in this part of England. The principal traffic was always freight, especially coal, with the result that
passenger traffic succumbed quite early, Heanor station being
closed as soon as 4th May 1926 and Butterley in 1947. Freight
traffic gradually diminished during the next thirty years and, after
British Rail withdrew, a group of Midland Railway enthusiasts
decided on a revival based on Butterley station. They worked to
such good effect that the Centre opened in May 1982. The site has
been gradually extended so that passengers are conveyed over a
route of approximately 4 miles (6.4 km). Visitors enter a train at
Butterley and proceed to Swanwick Junction. The next stop in the
eastwards direction is Riddings, where the locomotive runs round

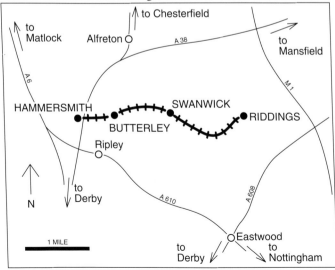

Midland Railway Centre. BR Standard class 4 2-6-4T no. 80080 and LMR class 5 4-6-0 no. 44767 crossing Butterley Reservoir with a restaurant car train.

the train to take it back to Swanwick. The train then runs through Butterley to the terminus at Hammersmith, and finally the journey ends at Butterley.

The ticket-holder is allowed to make an unlimited number of journeys in the day, but there is a large number of attractions on site. Trains run throughout the year but the best services are from April to October. At peak there are nine trains daily and the Centre offers meals on the move. Sunday lunches, afternoon teas, children's parties and evening specials can all be booked. The visitor will find many items of interest. There is a narrow-gauge line (2 feet, 610 mm), called the Golden Valley Railway, running from the Centre to the country park, which is suitable for picnics, and on Sundays during the summer trains run on the Butterley Park miniature railway (gauges $3^{1}/_{2}$ and 5 inches; 89 and 127 mm). In addition to refreshment rooms, there are the Matthew Kirtley Museum, the Road Transport Gallery, the Historic Carriage Workshop and the usual shop. The Midland Railway atmosphere is emphasised by the preservation of the former signal boxes of Kettering, Ais Gill, Kilby Bridge and Linby. Each year there are no fewer than thirty-four special events. Thomas the Tank Engine appears on four occasions, and there are the usual Santa Specials at Christmas, followed by Mince Pie Specials.

The Centre has a fascinating collection of steam, diesel and electric power, much of it on display in the museum building. Locomotives in service include LMS 4-6-2 no. 46208 *Princess Margaret Rose,* LMS 4-6-0 no. 44932, LMS 0-6-0Ts nos. 47327 and 47357, BR Co-Co no. 55015 *Tulyar,* and BR 1Co-Co1 no. 40012 *Aureol.*

The Centre is maintained by the Midland Railway Trust Ltd.

36. Nene Valley Railway

Headquarters. Wansford station, Stibbington, Peterborough. Telephone: 01780 782854.
Origin. Northampton & Peterborough Railway: opened 1845, closed 1957.

The Northampton & Peterborough Railway was worked from the start by the London & Birmingham Railway (which became the London & North Western Railway in July 1846). The town of Peterborough was of growing importance in the 1840s and it was natural that the London & Birmingham Railway should wish to be the first on the scene. They were followed by the Eastern Counties Railway in 1847 with their line from Ely, and in 1848 the Midland ran trains from Leicester over the new Syston & Peterborough Railway. The LNWR and the ECR were very sensitive to the competition to be offered by the London & York Railway and that is why they so bitterly opposed the L&YR Bill in the Commons in 1845. But the London & York was successful, and when it amalgamated with the Direct Northern in March 1846 to found the Great Northern, they were again successful in June 1846 with the Great Northern Bill. As the distance from Maiden Lane, the London terminus of the GNR, to Peterborough was only 76 miles (122 km), as compared with the LNWR mileage of 110 (177 km) from

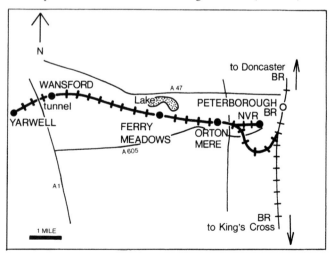

Nene Valley Railway. German Federal Railways 2-6-2T no. 64.305 coupled to Danish State Railway 0-6-0T no. 656 at Wansford.

Euston via Northampton, it is easy to understand why the latter were so concerned. The Eastern Counties route via Ely from Bishopsgate was 99½ miles (160 km). In 1845 the L&BR had supported a proposed line from Bletchley to Wellingborough via Newport Pagnell as this, by joining the N&PR at Wellingborough, would have cut their mileage from London to Peterborough to 90 (145 km). The plan was dropped as soon as Parliament approved the GNR Bill.

However, the N&PR became a very important cross-country route because it linked Birmingham, Coventry and Rugby with the east coast and its important nineteenth-century ports. At the same time there was useful local traffic between the towns of Wellingborough, Thrapston and Oundle. When the Midland extended its railway from Wigston Junction to Hitchin in 1857, they put in a link at Wellingborough to join the stations later known as Wellingborough Midland Road and London Road respectively.

At the turn of the century passenger traffic was handled by 'Jumbo' 2-4-0s and goods by 'Cauliflower' 0-6-0s. By 1939 there had been a change to the Midland class 2 4-4-0s and 'Super D' 0-8-0s, and in the last days of the LMS the Black 5s and the Stanier 8s were in evidence. In the final days before closure there were the usual BR standard mixed traffic classes, and often a speedy

Nene Valley Railway. Swedish State Railway 2-6-2T no. 1178 running round its train at Peterborough (Nene Valley station).

Thompson B1.

The loss of so important a line roused the local enthusiasts to action but it was not until 1968 that the Peterborough Railway Society was able to become an effective force and, as usual, a railway company had to be formed for the transfer of the Light Railway Order. This was called the Nene Valley Railway, appropriately, and it dates from 1973. Much hard labour was performed to restore the track, so that by 1974 a few trains ran, to be followed by a regular service in 1977.

Train services are now provided at weekends from February to December, also on Wednesdays after Easter, and six days a week in August. There are 'Thomas' events in June and August, and Santa Specials in December. The company is now operating a number of freight trains. The journey from Wansford (where there are shops and refreshment rooms) is through the pretty Nene Park, laid out by the Peterborough Corporation; the stations are Yarwell, Wansford, Ferry Meadows, Orton Mere and Peterborough (NVR). The total distance is 7 miles (11 km). The possibilities of an extension of the railway to Oundle are being considered.

One of the most interesting features of the Nene Valley Railway is its ability to accept rolling stock of the Berne loading gauge, and this was made possible by the decision to set back the platform faces slightly. Thus the company has built up a wonderful collection of foreign locomotives as shown below. British-built rolling stock has been fitted with slightly wider footboards to compensate.

The locomotives include: SR 4-6-2 no. 34081 *92 Squadron*; Swedish State 2-6-2T no. 1178 (1914); German Federal 2-6-2T by Krupp no. 64305 (1934); and Danish 0-6-0T no. 656. There are also Swedish B class 4-6-0 no. 1697, dating from 1943, Danish S class 2-6-4T no. 740 of 1925 manufacture, BR diesel nos. 55022 *Royal Scots Grey* and 55016 *Gordon Highlander*. There is also an industrial 0-6-0ST *Jacks Green* but probably the most important is BR Standard class 5 4-6-0 no. 73050, as this engine started the whole preservation scheme for the NVR.

The railway has another great attraction in its Italian-built Wagon Restaurant no. 2975; there is some Danish rolling stock and some SR stock. Two other items must be mentioned: at Wansford a 60 foot (18 metre) turntable and the largest preserved signal box in Britain.

The Continental Locomotive Group has purchased steam locomotive no. 740.161 from the Italian State Railways; it is proposed to run it on the Nene Valley Railway, thus further enriching the collection of foreign rolling stock.

Apart from the railway, Wansford has claims on the visitor: a beautiful church and the famous Haycock Inn. And who, being so near Peterborough, could resist seeing the splendid cathedral?

37. North Norfolk Railway

Headquarters. Sheringham station, Sheringham, Norfolk NR26 8RA. Telephone: 01263 822045; (timetable) 01263 825449.
Origin. Midland & Great Northern Joint Railway: opened at various dates between 1858 and 1894, closed 1959.

The constituents of the M&GNJR were many and varied, and the various amalgamations make a most interesting but complicated story. Excellent books have been written on the subject, describing how the Norwich & Spalding (1862), the Peterborough Wisbech & Sutton (1866) and the Eastern & Midlands (1866) joined forces. Some lines had been worked from the start either by the Midland or by the Great Northern so that the actual takeover was only a matter of time. The two large companies created the Midland & Great Northern Joint Railway in 1893. The line with which we are concerned, Holt to Cromer, had been opened in the meantime (June 1887). The closure of such a long section of main line on 28th February 1959 came as a shock to railway travellers as it was the first of several, and it was seven years before similar sentences were passed on the Somerset & Dorset Joint and the Great Central. It is so often overlooked by enthusiasts that the most effective way of preventing closures is not by protesting but by the habitual purchase of railway tickets. The M&GNJR had served the Midlands and East Anglia very well but the day came when the handsome locomotives were seen no more in mustard livery.

The Midland & Great Northern Joint Railway Society was first formed in 1960, soon after closure, but the difficulties in obtaining sufficient support and finance to revive the line seemed enormous.

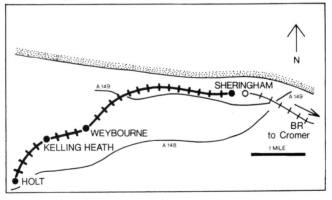

North Norfolk Railway. LNER J15 0-6-0 (GER Y14) with a train from Sheringham to Weybourne.

The reconstitution of the society in 1967 led to the formation of the North Norfolk Railway in 1970.

The Society decided, rightly, to make a modest start and to reopen 3 miles (4.8 km) of track between Sheringham and Weybourne. There were special difficulties in acquiring Sheringham station, but when this was achieved, and the usual labour of clearing the track and installing signalling had been done, the way was open for the first train, which ran in 1976. The enthusiasm of members has made the reopening possible and the prosperity of the NNR is also due to the very pretty scenery along the line, which has made it possible to attract over 100,000 passengers a year. Broadly speaking, the services are at weekends from March to October, increasing to daily in July, August and September. The locomotive shed is at Weybourne station and there are a shop, restaurant and museum at Sheringham. Both Sheringham and Weybourne stations are very attractive in design and have been restored. In August 1983 the railway was extended to Kelling Heath and in 1987 to Holt.

Steam locomotives include a class J94 Hunslet (Giesl) 0-6-0ST (3809/1954), another 0-6-0ST, *Ring Haw*, from Hunslet and an Andrew Barclay 0-6-0ST no.100 *Harlaxton*. Diesel power is represented by *Dr Harry*, a Ruston & Hornsby 0-4-0 shunter (1962), BR class 27 diesel locomotive D5386 and by German-built railcar no. 79963.

Coaching stock includes a Gresley 'Quad' set and a London & Northern Western Railway directors' saloon. Like other preserved railways, the NNR has been the scene of several films, and Weybourne was once covered with artificial snow for this purpose (*Fall of Eagles*).

After exceptional difficulties to begin with, the officials of both the Society and the railway must feel very satisfied with the position today.

North Staffordshire Railway. The Churnet Valley line of the NSR was famous for its beautiful stations. This is the attractive stone building at Cheddleton, looking towards Leek in 1973. The single line for mineral traffic was closed by British Rail on 30th August 1988.

38. North Staffordshire Railway Company (1978) Ltd

Headquarters. Cheddleton Railway Centre, Cheddleton station, Leek, Staffordshire. Telephone: 01538 360522 or 01782 503458.
Origin. Churnet Valley Railway: opened 13th July 1849; closed, North Rode to Leek, 7th November 1960; Leek to Uttoxeter, 4th January 1965.

The Churnet Valley Railway had obtained powers to build its line in 1846, but in 1847 it joined with two others to become the North Staffordshire Railway. The railway was known as the 'Knotty' as its coat of arms included the Staffordshire Knot. The engineer, George Parker Bidder, built an excellent line which ran through attractive scenery. The station buildings are notable for their architectural excellence. The North Staffordshire Railway was famous for its independent spirit and, in contrast to the North London Railway and the Lancashire & Yorkshire Railway, it maintained its integrity until the Grouping of 1923. In 1922, the last year of the Knotty's independent working, there were five trains daily between Macclesfield and Uttoxeter, and seven in the reverse direction. These were reduced to two each way on Sundays. Another North Staffordshire service was from Leek to Waterhouses, where the passenger could change on to the Leek & Manifold Light Railway. This line was laid to a gauge of 2 feet 6 inches (762 mm) and ran 8 miles (12.8 km) to its terminus at Hulme End. This railway was opened on 27th June 1904 and proved to be very popular as it ran through country of outstanding beauty. Road traffic affected its prosperity and it closed on 12th March 1934.

A railway preservation society was formed in 1971 and its efforts were concentrated on Cheddleton station, and since 1976 the Cheddleton Railway Centre has flourished. The station buildings here are very fine and it is pleasant to record that Sir John Betjeman was instrumental in preventing demolition by British Rail. There is plenty to interest the public at Cheddleton. In addition to the station building, reputed to be designed by Pugin, there are refreshment rooms, a shop, car park and picnic site beside the river Churnet. There is an excellent small exhibits museum and a working signal box can be visited. But the chief attraction at the Centre must be the train rides provided over a very long siding. There is a variety of entertainment during the year: a model railway day in June, and in July and August visits by Thomas the Tank Engine. For children there is a Teddy Bears' Picnic in

August, and in December the usual Santa Specials. The Centre is open to visitors on Sundays and bank holiday Mondays.

The locomotive stock is of great interest. There are the following steam engines: 'Austerity' 0-6-0ST *Josiah Wedgwood*, British Rail class 4 2-6-4T no. 80136, LMS class 4 0-6-0 no. 4422, and NSR 0-6-2T no. 2 (on loan from the National Railway Museum). There are also several former British Rail diesels: class 03 shunter no. 03 2070; class 08 shunter no. 3420; class 25 no. 7672 *Tamworth Castle*; and no. 33102.

Obviously the North Staffordshire Railway Company (1978) Ltd wished to expand their operations beyond Cheddleton station, but they were hampered by the fact that British Rail continued to use the section from Oakamoor Quarry to Leekbrook Junction and

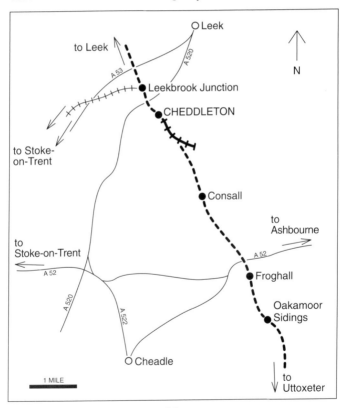

North Staffordshire Railway. L class 0-6-2T locomotive no. 2, seen standing on new trackwork to the south of Cheddleton. This engine is the sole survivor of the locomotive stock of the former North Staffordshire Railway.

on to Stoke-on-Trent for their stone trains. This traffic ceased on 30th August 1988 and negotiations began regarding the purchase of the track and equipment applicable thereto. The object is to acquire 7 miles (11 km) of railway extending from Leekbrook Junction to Oakamoor Sidings, and to raise the necessary money a new company has been formed – Churnet Valley Railway (1992) plc. In addition to funds arising from the issue of shares, there has been considerable support from local firms, the Cheddleton Parish Council and the Museums and Galleries Commission. Further support is promised by the Staffordshire Moorlands District Council. The successful outcome of this flotation will mean a valuable addition to the world of preserved railways.

39. North Yorkshire Moors Railway

Headquarters. Trust Office, Pickering station, Pickering, North Yorkshire YO18 7AJ. Telephone: 01751 472508; (talking time-table) 01751 473535.

Origin. Whitby & Pickering Railway: opened 1836, closed 1965.

Trains commenced running on the Whitby & Pickering Railway, drawn by horses, only eleven years after the opening of the Stockton & Darlington Railway. However, the horses could not manage the whole distance as there was an incline about 1 mile (1.6 km) in length with a gradient of 1 in 15. This lay between Beck Hole and Goathland and was worked by cable. With steam railways spreading all over Britain it was obvious that the horses would be displaced. This occurred soon after the York & North Midland Railway bought up the Whitby & Pickering; the steep incline was bypassed and by 1847 steam engines worked through the whole distance. This improvement was due to the energy of George Hudson, whose York & North Midland and York Newcastle & Berwick railways opened the north-east of England to rail transport. So much can be charged against Hudson that it is pleasant to be able to say something to his credit, and surely the creation of

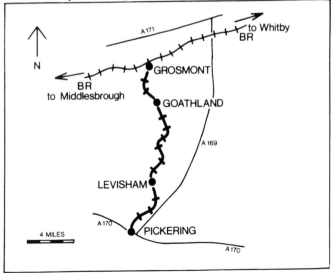

90

North Yorkshire Moors Railway. The 15.50 train from Grosmont to Pickering going well behind Southern Railway class S15 4-6-0 no. 841 'Greene King'.

the Midland Railway in 1844 and the North Eastern in 1854 are memorials to his ability. Although he had left the railway world in 1849, the NER was made possible by his system of amalgamations.

The line was expensive to work as it included a gradient of 1 in 49, and it lay through sparsely inhabited country. Today it might well be regarded as having sufficient social purpose to be kept open, but the Beeching Report of 1963 was obsessed with profit making and it could not pardon such a branch as the Whitby & Pickering. We must therefore be grateful to the North Yorkshire Moors Railway Preservation Society, formed in 1967 for the purpose of revitalising 18 miles (29 km) of the railway. The society was succeeded by the North York Moors Historical Railway Trust, which worked to such good purpose that the first train ran in 1973.

This long preserved railway runs through countryside of outstanding beauty and the gradients call for hard work from the locomotives. Services are operated daily from March to November, with 'Santa Specials' in December. The North York Moors Railway is therefore well able to attract the public, which it does at an annual figure of 250,000 passengers. The stations are Grosmont (pronounced 'Gromont'), Goathland, Levisham and Pickering. All have refreshment facilities except Levisham.

In 1923, when the London & North Eastern Railway was formed, its most important member was the North Eastern Railway, which paid the highest dividends and had the most powerful locomotives. It is therefore fitting that the NYMR possesses two fine specimens of NER design, as will be seen in the following list. The diesel locomotives are essential if a dry summer makes the use of spark-throwing steam engines inadvisable in the wooded sections of the line. There are fully equipped workshops for maintaining the locomotives.

Steam locomotives are: NER T2 0-8-0 no. 2238, P3 0-6-0 no. 2392 and T3 no. 901; LNER K1 2-6-0 no. 2005 (Thompson design); LMS Black 5 nos. 4767 *George Stephenson* and 5428 *Eric Treacey*; SR S15 4-6-0 no. 841, 'Schools' class 4-4-0 no. 926 *Repton* and 'West Country' 4-6-2 no. 34010 *Sidmouth*; GWR 0-6-2T no. 6619; WD 2-10-0 no. 601; 'Austerity' 0-6-0ST no. 75130; BR Standard class 4 2-6-4T no. 80135, class 4 4-6-0 no. 75014; Lambton Colliery 0-6-2T no. 29. Diesel locomotives are: class 24 no. D5032, and 'Deltic' no. 55009 *Alycidon*.

Paignton & Dartmouth Railway. GWR 2-6-2T no. 4555 on an up train crosses GWR 2-8-0T no. 5239 on a down train at Churston.

40. Paignton & Dartmouth Railway

Headquarters. Queens Park station, Torbay Road, Paignton, Devon
TQ4 6AF. Telephone: 01803 555872.

Origin. Dartmouth & Torbay Railway, opened Torquay to Paignton
1859, to Brixham Road 1861, and to Kingswear 1864; branch
from Churston Ferrers to Brixham 1865; broad gauge 1859 to
1892, standard gauge till closure in 1972.

In order to provide a coast route in south Devon between Exeter
and Plymouth an engineer would have to negotiate four rivers, the
Teign, Dart, Avon and Erme. It is hardly surprising therefore to
find that Brunel chose to go inland, although the line necessitated
heavy gradients, partly because, at the time, he was a convert to the
atmospheric system of traction. The important town of Dartmouth
found that it had a railway station no nearer than Totnes, about 9
miles (14 km) in a direct line although 14 miles (23 km) by the
existing roads. A fresh railway was clearly necessary, but the
promoters of the Dartmouth & Torbay decided to keep to the east
of the river Dart, and the terminus proved to be at Kingswear, thus
forcing the traveller to cross over to Dartmouth by ferry. This
position never changed, so Dartmouth was always without a railway station. The new line progressed as indicated in the heading. A
year after the trains reached Kingswear, a company called the
Torbay & Brixham Railway opened its branch from Brixham Road
to Brixham, when the former station was renamed Churston.
Bradshaw's *Railway Manual* refers to this place as 'Churston
Ferrers'. Railways like these, far removed from industrial England, would derive their income partly from shipping, but more
and more from holiday traffic as time passed. This source of
revenue was sensitive to road competition but closure did not come
until 1972, a full twenty years after a whole series of closures by
the British Transport Commission.

It was most fortunate that the former Dart Valley Railway had
had ten years' experience by 1972 and it purchased the Dartmouth
& Torbay Railway before deterioration could set in. Thus the old
Great Western is gloriously revived in this area, both by the former
Dart Valley Railway (now the South Devon Railway – see page
107) and the former Torbay & Dartmouth Railway (now the
Paignton & Dartmouth Railway). Further support for the GWR is
found at Didcot, where the Great Western Society thrives, and on
the Severn Valley and West Somerset railways. Since 1972 a
service of trains has been built up so that between Easter and
October they run daily. There are also Santa Specials at Christmas.

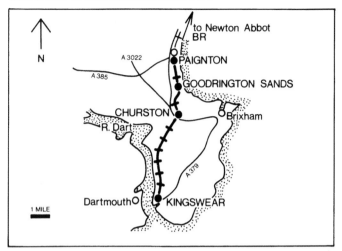

As one would expect from a Devon railway, the scenery is delightful and the sea appears first on the east and then on the west. The stations are Paignton, Goodrington Sands, Churston, and Kingswear. Paignton has a refreshment room and a shop selling books and souvenirs. In the yard is a locomotive depot where engines are kept up to concert pitch. The stock of locomotives is truly representative of the former Great Western Railway: 2-6-2Ts nos. 4555 and 4588; 4-6-0 no. 7827 *Lydham Manor*; and the powerful 2-8-0T no. 5239.

Some of the coaches are of GWR origin and all are finished in the splendid chocolate and cream livery which matches so well the Brunswick green of the locomotives. The trains therefore have a 1939 look about them.

41. Ravenglass & Eskdale Railway

Headquarters. Ravenglass, Cumbria. Telephone: 01229 717171.
Origin. Eskdale iron mines 3 foot (913 mm) gauge railway: opened
  1876, closed 1912.

A railway built specially to convey iron ore from the mines to a
railhead or port can last only as long as the ore exists. This is what
happened to the original line and closure came in 1912. After
three years a firm called Narrow Gauge Railways Ltd bought the
buildings and track and decided to lay an entirely new railway
with a gauge of 15 inches (381 mm). The locomotives were built
by Bassett Lowke Ltd of Northampton, who specialised in this
type of work. These beautiful engines, made almost exactly to
scale, were not as robust as the ones bought from a private railway
in Derbyshire and were duly withdrawn. The railway changed
hands twice before the owners, now the Keswick Granite Company, closed it in 1958 for the second time. A preservation society
was formed and it was decided to run trains for passengers only.
The administration is by a manager with a small permanent staff
for operation and the latter are assisted by volunteers from the
R&ER Preservation Society.

The journey from Ravenglass to Dalegarth is through superb
scenery, the distance being nearly 7 miles (11 km). The stations are
Ravenglass, Muncaster Mill, Irton Road, The Green, Beckfoot,
and Dalegarth. There are stretches at a gradient of 1 in 42. Train
services are daily from Easter to October.

As might be expected, the steam locomotives are very robust and
have no difficulty in performing their onerous duties. Among them

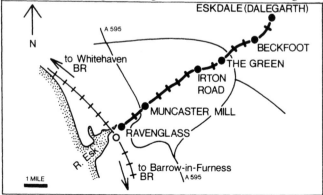

Ravenglass & Eskdale Railway. 2-8-2 'River Esk' arriving at Dalegarth on the 14.40 from Ravenglass.

are 0-8-2 *River Irt*, 2-8-2 *River Esk*, 2-8-2 *River Mite*, 2-6-2 *Northern Rock*, 0-4-2 *Bonnie Dundee* and diesel locomotives 2-6-2 *Shelagh of Eskdale* and BB *Lady Wakefield*.

At Ravenglass there are shops and refreshment rooms. There is also a museum, which houses, among other items, a 1912-built Bassett Lowke 4-4-2.

42. Romney Hythe & Dymchurch Railway

Headquarters. New Romney Station, New Romney, Kent TN28 8PL. Telephone: 01797 362353 or 363256.
Origin. 15 inch (381 mm) gauge railway laid down for Captain J. E. P. Howey in the years 1925-8.

A purist might rightly argue that this railway, having never closed down completely, therefore cannot be said to be 'preserved'. But the RH&DR, like many other lines, has known financial difficulty and has been saved by wise management. In this sense it could be called a preserved railway. The construction of the railway was commissioned by Captain Howey in 1925 after he acquired two part-built 15 inch (381 mm) gauge Pacific-type locomotives that had been ordered by his friend Count Louis Zbrowski. Unfortunately the Count was killed whilst racing at Monza and Howey took over the locomotives and looked for somewhere to run them. Together with the engineer Henry Greenly, he eventually settled on a line between Hythe and New Romney along the coast of Romney Marsh in Kent. This double-track line opened in 1927 and the following year was extended to Dungeness to make a total length of 13$\frac{1}{2}$ miles (22 km). The railway's title, although not geographically correct, does mention the three principal stations of the original line.

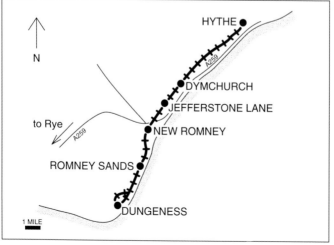

Romney Hythe & Dymchurch Railway. 4-8-2 no. 5 'Hercules' at New Romney shed. It is difficult to realise that the gauge is 15 inches (381 mm).

The railway prospered in the pre-war years, mainly owing to the large number of holiday camps that sprang up in this coastal area. During the Second World War the railway played its part in the defence of the south coast when it was taken over by the army. A miniature armoured train, troop trains and supply trains kept the railway busy until it was taken over by the Ministry of Works to be used in the construction of the petrol pipeline (PLUTO) under the Channel. In 1945 the railway was handed back to Captain Howey and was reopened to passengers in 1946.

There is a daily service from Easter to the end of September and a weekend service during March and October. Hythe station is about 2 miles (3 km) from Junction 11 off the M20 whilst most of the other stations are on or near the A259 south coast trunk road. Since the closure of New Romney and Hythe British Rail stations the best way to get to the railway by public transport is to take a train to Folkestone Central and then a bus to Hythe.

The principal stations are Hythe, Dymchurch, Jefferstone Lane (for St Mary's Bay), New Romney, Romney Sands and Dungeness. The train, when approaching Dungeness, negotiates spring points, taking the left-hand road to Dungeness station. On leaving the station the train continues round the loop and through the spring points to regain its former track to Hythe. There are cafes at

Dungeness and New Romney stations, a fine toy and model museum at New Romney with a large automatic 00 gauge railway layout, picnic sites and gift and souvenir shops. The railway has a very loyal following amongst the public and regularly carries 140,000 passengers a year.

The RH&DR shares a common gauge with several other railways and locomotives are occasionally exchanged on a temporary basis. In recent years this has included visiting engines from as far away as California and Tasmania.

The scenery around the RH&DR could be said to be unique. Starting from alongside the picturesque Royal Military Canal at Hythe, the line runs through an ever changing landscape of housing developments, fine farmland populated with sheep and cattle, small villages and historic churches until it finally reaches the vast shingle wastes of Dungeness.

The RH&DR still possesses all its original locomotives. Although not scale models, all of the British outline locomotives have a definite 'Gresley' feel to them, whilst the Canadian-style locomotives would look just as much at home on the North American prairies as they do on the Romney Marsh. The following are in service (4-6-2 type unless otherwise shown): no. 1 *Green Goddess*, no. 2 *Northern Chief*, no. 3 *Southern Maid*, no. 5 *Hercules* (4-8-2), no. 6 *Samson* (4-8-2), no. 7 *Typhoon*, no. 8 *Hurricane*, no. 9 *Churchill* (Canadian style), no. 10 *Dr Syn* (Canadian style), no. 11 *Black Prince* (German style). In addition there is the 0-4-0 shunting loco *The Bug* and two diesel locomotives, no. 12 *John Southland* and no. 14 *Captain Howey*. There are also three small internal combustion locomotives used for yard and permanent way work. Most of the passenger stock consists of enclosed bogie coaches although there are also some open and semi-open coaches as well.

43. Severn Valley Railway

Headquarters. The Railway Station, Bewdley, Worcestershire DY12 1BG. Telephone: 01299 403816; (talking timetable) 01299 401001.
Origin. Severn Valley Railway: opened 1862, closed 1963.

From its opening date the original Severn Valley Railway was worked by the West Midland Railway. The latter had a most extraordinary history even for the mid nineteenth century, which abounded in bizarre companies. In 1845 an Act was secured by the Oxford Worcester & Wolverhampton Railway to construct a network of lines between those three cities, it being stipulated that the tracks should be laid to mixed gauge (4 feet 8^1/$_2$ inches and 7 feet 0^1/$_4$ inch – 1436 mm and 2140 mm). At stations the rail nearest the platform was common to both gauges. The OW&WR soon exhausted its capital and Captain Simmonds, the Board of Trade inspector, informed the Railway Commissioners that the company need another £850,000 to complete its work. A fresh Act (1850) gave the necessary powers, and by 1852 the Midland was working the OW&WR trains between Worcester and Droitwich. These trains obviously ran on the standard-gauge track and, although the outer rail had been laid, no points or junctions connecting it had been supplied. For this reason the Great Western refused to have anything to do with the OW&WR. Further strength was given to the standard-gauge network when the London & North Western Railway laid a connection from Banbury Road junction (near

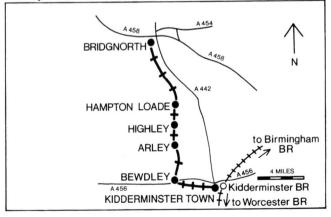

100

Oxford) to Yarnton in 1854. The GWR was still unable to run its trains over the OW&WR but the two companies signed an agreement in 1858 to the effect that neither would support any line which might damage the other's interests without prior consultation.

The Oxford Worcester & Wolverhampton Railway was not very prosperous, and it would have welcomed a takeover either by the LNWR or the GWR. In 1860, to strengthen its position, it amalgamated with two smaller companies to become the West Midland Railway, and two years later it began to work the trains over the Severn Valley Railway, which had opened in February 1862. The service was from Shrewsbury to Bewdley, Hartlebury, Droitwich and Worcester. In 1857 the Wycombe Railway, a small but ambitious company, had obtained an Act to build a line from Princes Risborough to Oxford, and immediately the OW&WR saw in this an opportunity to goad the GWR into action. The Wycombe Railway commenced running to Oxford in 1862, and in that year the WMR accused the GWR of violating the agreement of 1858. In order to bring matters to a head, the WMR proposed an entirely new company, the London Buckinghamshire & West Midland

Severn Valley Railway. BR Standard class 4 4-6-0 no. 75069 at Arley on the 12.19 train to Kidderminster Town on 15th May 1990.

Junction Railway, which would build a line from Yarnton to London via Thame, Wendover and Uxbridge. This obvious threat to the GWR was not lost on the larger company, and when the LNWR hinted that it would support the LB&WMJR the Great Western amalgamated with the West Midland. Thus the smaller company achieved its object, and in due course the GWR worked the Severn Valley, absorbing it in 1872.

The closure of the SVR in 1963 as part of the Beeching 'Reshaping of the Railways' resulted in the formation of the Severn Valley Railway Society in 1966, and in 1970 it was announced that trains were to run between Bridgnorth and Hampton Loade. The line was gradually extended until today it has a total of 16 miles (25.6 km) between Bridgnorth and Kidderminster.

The SVR runs trains at weekends throughout the year, and daily from May to October. As the track runs alongside the river Severn for the whole of the journey the traveller is enabled to see some outstanding scenery and the notable Victoria Bridge across the Severn at Arley. The SVR attracts 180,000 passengers a year. A feature which should not be missed is the Sunday lunch trains which run on most Sundays throughout the year. There are Santa Specials on Saturdays and Sundays in December. The stations are Bridgnorth, Hampton Loade, Highley, Arley, Bewdley and Kidderminster Town.

Owing to its excellent workshops, the company has been able to own or to attract a large number of interesting locomotives. They are as follows: GWR 4-6-0 nos. 7802 *Bradley Manor* and 7812 *Erlestoke Manor*, 0-6-0PT no. 1501 (Hawksworth design with outside cylinders), 2-6-2T no. 4150, 2-6-0 no. 7325, 2-6-2T nos. 5164 and 4566, 4-6-0 nos. 6960 *Raveningham Hall*, 4930 *Hagley Hall* and 7819 *Hinton Manor*; LMS Black 5 no. 45110 *RAF Biggin Hill*, 8F 2-8-0 no. 8233, 2-6-0 nos. 43106, 46443, 42968 and 46521; LMR 0-6-0T 47383; WR 0-6-0PTs 7714 and 5764; BR Standard class 4 4-6-0 75069, class 2 2-6-0 78019 and class 4 2-6-4T 80079; and former Longmoor Military Railway 2-10-0 no. 600 *Gordon*. The LNER is represented by 60009 *Union of South Africa* and 2-6-0 no. 3442 *The Great Marquess*. There are several industrial tank engines and two of the celebrated 'Western' class diesel locomotives, D1013 *Western Ranger* and D1062 *Western Courier,* as well as three Class 50 locomotives, 'Warship' no. D821 *Greyhound,* plus representatives of Class 25 and 27.

Bridgnorth has an interesting church and several inns of architectural merit.

44. Sittingbourne & Kemsley Light Railway

Headquarters. Sittingbourne, Kent. Telephone: 01634 852672.
Origin. Edward Lloyd & Company, Sittingbourne Paper Mill, opened 1906.

Edward Lloyd & Company built a railway of 2 feet 6 inches (762 mm) gauge to serve their works internally so that materials and equipment could be moved with the greatest ease. After 1918 the line was extended to Ridham Dock on the river Swale, thus allowing the firm direct access to shipping. After thirty years, Edward Lloyd was taken over by the Bowater Group and the short railway became very busy. In 1965 the group decided to change over to road haulage and offered the railway to the Locomotive Club of Great Britain. The company, which is now serarate from the LCGB, operates 2 miles (3.2 km) of track, and the reconstituted light railway dates from 1969. There is a service of trains from Easter to mid October on Sundays and bank holiday Mondays and

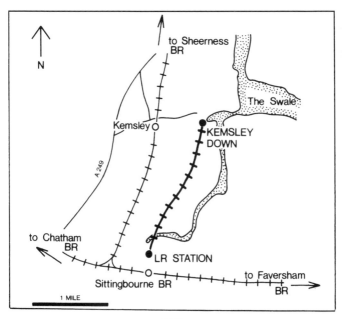

on Wednesdays and Saturdays in August. The work of operating is carried out by volunteers among the company members. The stations are Sittingbourne (near the Railtrack station) and Kemsley Down.

The locomotives present an interesting appearance as some of the chimneys are fitted with spark arresters owing to the combustible nature of the surroundings. The steam engines are: three 0-6-2Ts by Bagnall, named *Alpha*, *Triumph* and *Superb*; three 0-4-2STs by Kerr Stuart, named *Premier, Melior* and *Leader*; and a Bagnall fireless 2-4-0 *Unique,* which is non-operational. Diesel locomotives are a Hunslet, and a Ruston & Hornsby named *Edward Lloyd*. The rolling stock consists of workmen-type bogie coaches and a variety of goods wagons.

This short railway is well maintained, and as most of the steam locomotives have sand boxes mounted on the boiler, in addition to the spark arresters, there is a foreign ambience in the ride from Sittingbourne to Kemsley Down.

45. Snowdon Mountain Railway

Headquarters. Llanberis, Caernarfon LL55 4TY. Telephone: 01286 870223.
Origin. Snowdon Mountain Railway: opened 1895.

This railway, 4³/₄ miles (7.6 km) in length and having a gauge of 2 feet 7¹/₂ inches (800 mm), has been operating successfully since its inception. It is not therefore a preserved railway in the sense that others are but it cannot be omitted from this book because it is the only mountain railway in Britain worked on the Abt rack system. Obviously a line which climbs up to 3493 feet (1065 metres) can offer the traveller superb views, but there are two points which should not be overlooked. First, choose a fine day as it can be disappointing not to see anything but mountain mist; second, be sure to carry a coat to wear at the summit as naturally there is a considerable drop in temperature at such an altitude.

Trains run daily (weather permitting) from mid March through October although early and late season trains terminate at Rocky

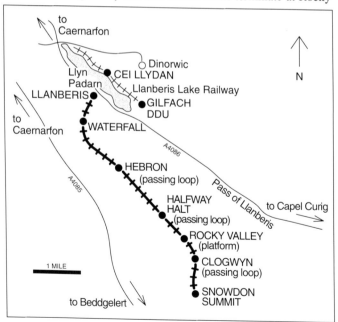

Valley or Clogwyn when snow and ice make the upper reaches of the line impassable. The stations are Llanberis, followed by several halts and finally the terminus at the summit of Snowdon. (Tickets are not normally issued to intermediate stations.) The stations at each end have refreshment rooms.

As Switzerland is the home of rack-operated railways it is not surprising that several of the locomotives are of Swiss manufacture. There are seven from the Winterthur locomotive works, built between 1895 and 1923, although it is now rare to find more than four in steam on any one day. As the engines perform so much of their work on a gradient of 1 in 6, the boilers have a slope down from the firebox to the smokebox, thus ensuring an even water level when the hard labour is being done on the steepest slopes. The coaching stock is mounted on bogies and affords adequate weather protection for the passenger.

The enthusiast for steam engines will revel in the roar of the exhaust for mile after mile. The journey takes about one hour in each direction, as stops must be made at the passing places. Four UK-built diesel locomotives have been acquired to supplement the services and are now the main workhorses of the locomotive fleet. The latest addition to the rolling stock is a three-car diesel-electric multiple-unit train, also UK-built.

South Devon Railway. GWR 2-6-2T no. 4555 leaving Buckfastleigh on the 15.00 train to Littlehempston.

46. South Devon Railway

Headquarters. Buckfastleigh, Devon. Telephone: 01364 642338.
Origin. Buckfastleigh, Totnes & South Devon Railway, opened
   1872, closed 1958 (Ashburton to Totnes).

The first line lay in Brunel's territory and was therefore a
broad-gauge railway (7 feet 0^1/$_4$ inch or 2140 mm). This great
engineer planned the South Devon Railway from Exeter to Plymouth but, having the atmospheric principle in mind, he permitted the gradients to be more severe than was customary for steam-
worked railways. The Ashburton branch left the main line at
Totnes and was worked by the South Devon Railway. The through
route to the west from Paddington was by the Great Western to
Bristol, then over the Bristol & Exeter Railway (opened in 1844)
and finally by means of the South Devon Railway (opened 1849).
The Great Western absorbed the B&ER in 1876 and the SDR in
1878.
   The Dart Valley Railway Society was formed in 1962 with the
object of purchasing the branch from Totnes to Ashburton and
operating it with a newly formed Dart Valley Railway. The
normal procedure was for British Rail to obtain a Light Railway
Order for working the line, after which the order would be transferred to the DVR. Unfortunately two unforeseen circumstances
affected this plan. The first was the building of the A38 trunk
road, which cut across the branch just north of Buckfastleigh
station. It was thus impossible to serve Ashburton. The second
was the refusal by British Rail to allow DVR trains to enter its
Totnes station, with the result that the DVR had to construct its
own station, Littlehempston Riverside. Nevertheless, a very fine
railway is now operating over the 5^1/$_2$ miles (8.9 km), the first
train departing in 1969. The railway has since changed its name
from the Dart Valley to the South Devon Railway. Services are
maintained at Easter, on Saturdays and Sundays in April, May and
October, and daily from mid May to September. Friends of Thomas appear in May and October and there are Santa Specials in
December.
   Refreshments may be obtained on Buckfastleigh station before
the traveller sets off for Littlehempston, stopping *en route* at
Staverton Bridge station. The line is a very pretty one as the
railway follows closely the course of the river Dart. The SDR
station at Totnes (Littlehempston) is reached via a fine new
footbridge near the mainline station.
   Locomotives tended to be J94 Austerity types in the early years

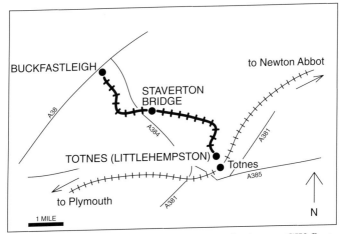

after the SDR takeover from DVLR but the line's own GW fleet, augmented by various visiting engines, is converting the line to its true GWR flavour. Locomotives at present include J94s *Sapper, Errol Lonsdale* and *Glendower,* 0-6-0PT no. 1369, 0-4-2T no. 1420, 0-6-0PT no. 5786, and Standard class 4 2-6-4T no. 80064.

47. South Tynedale Railway

Headquarters. The Railway Station, Alston, Cumbria. Telephone: 01434 381696.
Origin. Haltwhistle & Nanthead Railway: opened 17th November 1852, closed 3rd May 1976.

On 26th August 1846 powers were obtained to construct a railway from Haltwhistle on the Newcastle & Carlisle Railway to Nanthead, a distance of 17 miles (27 km). The first section, from Haltwhistle to Shafthill, 4¹⁄₄ miles (6.8 km), was opened on 19th July 1851. A longer portion, that from Alston to Lambley (8³⁄₄ miles, 14 km), enjoyed a train service from 5th January 1852, but the difficulty of the terrain required an expensive viaduct over the South Tyne river. When this work was completed the whole branch from Haltwhistle to Alston was opened on 17th November 1852. Lack of funds caused the abandonment of the section from Alston to Nanthead, the Lambley viaduct having proved very expensive. Two years after the opening, the great North Eastern Railway was created and most of the railways in the district were absorbed, but the absorption of the Alston branch did not take place until 1862.

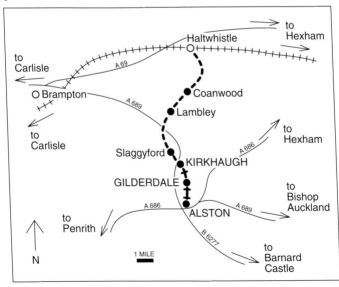

South Tynedale Railway. Diesel locomotive no. 1 waiting at Gilderdale for departure for Alston.

Throughout its existence the railway enjoyed a modest prosperity and was important to the district in winter when the roads were often blocked by snow. The withdrawal of services by British Rail was in reverse of the usual order, that is to say freight traffic ceased before passenger services. For some time trains were hauled by BR Standard class 3 2-6-0s (77000), and later, in an effort to reduce costs, the stations became unstaffed halts served by diesel multiple-unit trains. Unfortunately the end came on 3rd May 1976.

The closure of the last colliery in the district in 1956 was a severe blow to the freight traffic although goods trains continued to run until 1965. The branch had several viaducts, the maintenance of which would not be regarded favourably by British Rail.

The South Tynedale Railway Preservation Society was formed as early as 1973, as soon as the branch line was menaced with closure. The purchase of the railway was envisaged by the Society but the price required by British Rail was far too high. At a meeting of the society held at Haltwhistle in 1977 it was decided to invest in a narrow-gauge line (2 feet, 610 mm), and fortunately Cumbria County Council bought all the land from British Rail. The council then redeveloped Alston station site with the aid of the Manpower Services Commission, and a grant from the English Tourist Board made it possible for the first trains to run over a mile (1.6 km) of track on 30th July 1983. By 1987 the track had been extended to Gilderdale halt, a distance of 2 miles (3.2 km). A great deal of work has been done at Alston station. There are now maintenance workshops in the yard, and at the station itself a booking office, gift shop and information bureau. A signal box, which had stood at Ainderby near Northallerton, was bought from British Rail, dismantled and re-erected on the South Tynedale Railway. The line has reached Kirkhaugh, where a station has been built, and the intention is to reach Slaggyford and Lambley as soon as possible. A difficulty to be overcome is the repair work necessary on the Whitley viaduct.

Trains run during Easter week, each weekend in May, daily in June (except Mondays and Fridays), then every day in July and August. In September and October services are maintained daily (Mondays and Fridays excepted), and at weekends in November and December. Family attractions are Thomas the Tank Engine in May and October, Teddy Bear Day in June, with Santa and Mince Pie Specials in December.

The first locomotive arrived in August 1979, since when an interesting collection has been built up. These can be listed as follows: *Phoenix*, 40 horsepower diesel-mechanical; *Sao Domingos*, Orenstein & Koppel 0-6-0WT; *Naworth*, 100 horsepower Hudswell Clarke diesel-mechanical; *Thomas Edmondson*, Henschel 0-4-0T; Hunslet 70 horsepower diesel-mechanical; *Naklo*, Polish 0-6-0 tender/tank; *Cumbria*, Hunslet 60 horsepower diesel-mechanical; *Chaka's Kraal*, Hunslet 0-4-2T; *Helen Kathryn*, Henschel 0-4-0T.

There is an attractive collection of passenger vehicles, mostly in crimson lake livery.

48. Strathspey Railway

Headquarters. Aviemore Speyside station, Dalfaber Road, Aviemore, Inverness-shire PH22 1PY. Telephone: 01479 810725.
Origin. Inverness & Perth Junction Railway: opened 1863, closed 1965.

The Inverness & Perth Junction Railway was built to link the Inverness & Aberdeen Junction Railway at Forres to the Perth & Dunkeld Railway at Dunkeld to improve communications with the south. In 1865 these railways and others combined to form the Highland Railway Company, which had its headquarters in Inverness. In 1866 a company called the Strathspey Railway opened a line from Nethy Bridge to Boat of Garten (this was an extension of the line from Craigellachie to Nethy Bridge) to form a junction with the Highland at Boat of Garten. The Strathspey Railway was later absorbed by the Great North of Scotland Railway (which had its headquarters in Aberdeen). In 1898 the Highland Railway completed the new line from Aviemore to Inverness via Carrbridge and the Aviemore-Forres route became a secondary line. Along

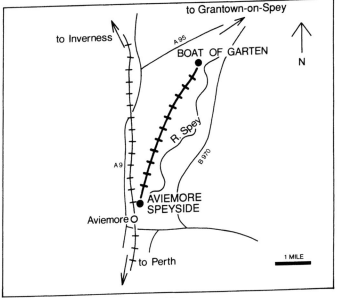

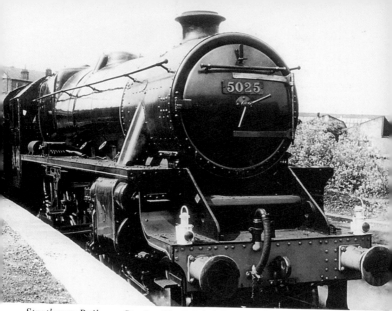

Strathspey Railway. Stanier Black 5 4-6-0 no. 5025. This locomotive was formerly on the Keighley & Worth Valley Railway.

with some other routes in the north of Scotland the Aviemore to Forres line was shut in the 1960s.

A scheme to preserve part of the line resulted in the formation of the Strathspey Railway Company Ltd in July 1971 and this band of enthusiasts managed to save 5 miles (8 km) of track from the scrap man. On 7th April 1973 the first train ran over the line under the auspices of the preservationists when a three-car diesel multiple unit ran an excursion from Edinburgh. The first steam passenger service was an LCGB special in September 1975, hauled by Black Five no. 5025. Public services began on 22nd July 1978, when 2-6-0 no. 46464 hauled the first train.

The railway operates services from Easter to October, running a daily service from June to September. Special events such as Friends of Thomas weekends (in May and September), an enthusiasts day (May) as well as Santa trains and Hogmanay specials in December are also operated. Morning coffee service and afternoon tea are offered on most days when steam trains run.

The railway is planning to move its Aviemore terminus to the mainline station in Aviemore and is working on extending the railway to Grantown-on-Spey. It is hoped that the first stage of the extension, the 4 miles (6 km) to Broomhill, will open in 1998.

Locomotives on the line include Black Five no. 5025 (built

1934), Ivatt 2-6-0 no. 46512 (currently undergoing restoration) and ex-Caledonian 812 class 0-6-0 no. 828. No. 828 is currently in use and displays the glorious blue Caley livery. Industrial types are represented by three Austerity 0-6-0ST tanks, and Barclay 0-6-0ST and 0-4-0ST tanks. Also on the railway are class 08, 26 and 27 diesel locomotives as well as a number of industrial diesel shunters. There are also two diesel multiple units. Coaching stock includes LMS, BR mark 1 and mark 2 coaches.

49. Swanage Railway

Headquarters. Station House, Swanage, Dorset. Telephone: 01929 425800.
Origin. London & South Western Railway branch: opened 1885, closed 3rd March 1972.

Like most railways in the south of England, the London & South Western Railway paid great attention to its passenger traffic because the conveyance of freight was on a much smaller scale than that of the northern companies. In its independent days the L&SWR ran nine expresses between Waterloo and Weymouth with connections for Swanage at Wareham. Four of these had refreshment cars. It is interesting to note that although passengers from London to Swanage had to change at Wareham those coming from Manchester had through carriages by one train a day in each direction. On the Swanage branch itself there were fifteen trains a day to and from Wareham – a very good service. The fastest time by steam train between Waterloo and Swanage was 3 hours 20 minutes, and although since 1994 the electric service has conveyed the passenger from London to Wareham in precisely two hours there is, unfortunately, no branch train. As the Swanage branch lasted until 1972 it was clearly not a victim of the Beeching plan. The real reason for closure was the private car.

The progress of the new Swanage Railway has been rapid. The first task was to restore Swanage station and engine shed and then to lay the track. By the summer of 1984 trains were running between Swanage and Herston, a distance of 2 miles (3.2 km). The next year the centenary of the branch was celebrated and an engine turntable was installed at Swanage. In 1988 the track had reached Harman's Cross. In 1995 Norden station was opened as the new terminus of the line. On the same date trains started running through Corfe Castle. The restoration of Swanage station was made possible by the dismantling and transfer of the original Dorchester South station. This had been in use from 1847 to 1969. During that period up trains had to run past the station and then back into it, but finally in 1969 British Rail rebuilt the station on more conventional lines.

The Swanage Railway is open to the public on Saturdays and Sundays in April and May, and daily from June until October. In November and December the line is open on Sundays only. There are the special days which are enjoyed on most preserved railways, for example Easter Egg trains and in May a Teddy Bears' Picnic. In October there is a visit by Thomas the Tank Engine, and in

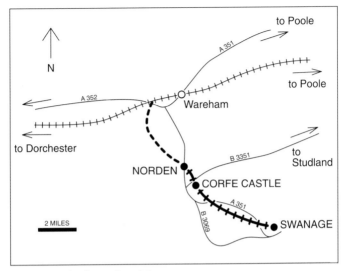

December the Santa Specials.

At Swanage there is an impressive collection of locomotives: Southern Railway 4-6-2 no. 35022 *Holland America Line*; GWR 0-6-2T no. 6695; Stanier 2-8-0 (from Turkey) no. 45160; BR Standard 2-6-4T no. 80078; Hunslet 0-6-0ST (1690/1931) *Cunarder*; and diesels class 25 no. 25244, Fowler shunter no. 2 *May* and BR class 08 no. 3591. To supplement steam there is a Gloucester Carriage & Wagon Company two-car diesel multiple-unit. Coaching stock includes a 1932 Pullman coach.

50. Swindon & Cricklade Railway

Headquarters. Railway Station, Tadpole Lane, Blunsdon, Swindon, Wiltshire. Telephone: 01793 771615.

Origin. Swindon & Cheltenham Extension Railway: opened 1891, closed 11th September 1961; Blunsdon station closed 1924.

The Swindon Marlborough & Andover Railway had been operating for ten years before the opening of the Swindon & Cheltenham Extension Railway, and the two companies soon amalgamated to form the Midland & South Western Junction Railway. The business of the M&SWJR was hampered between Marlborough and Savernake by the tactics of the Great Western Railway, as the former had to use GWR metals between these stations. However, the great Sam Fay, general manager of the M&SWJR, promoted the Marlborough & Grafton Railway Act so that after 1898 this obstruction was removed. In 1922, the last year of independent operation, the company ran four through trains daily between Cheltenham and Andover. It could be said that for twenty-five years the M&SWJR throve in a modest way. Under the provisions of the Railways Act 1921 the Midland & South Western Junction Railway was absorbed by the Great Western, hardly a promising future for the smaller company. Although traffic was reduced by the GWR, conditions became much worse under nationalisation

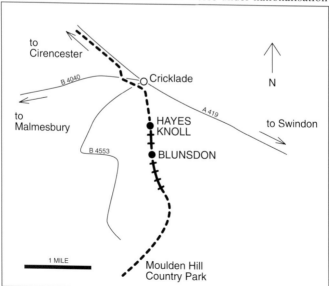

Swindon & Cricklade Railway. Barclay 0-4-0ST 'Richard Trevithick' with a train at Blunsdon station.

and by 1961 there was only one through train from Cheltenham to Andover.

It is interesting to note the revival of traffic at Blunsdon by the Swindon & Cricklade Railway, seeing that this station was closed in 1924. The M&SWJR had provided one platform and a siding at Blunsdon but in later years only one train stopped there. This was the 17.00 from Cricklade (Sundays only) arriving at Blunsdon at 17.15 and Swindon Town at 17.40. Presumably its leisurely progress was due to shunting at stations.

Since 1984 much hard work has been performed by members of the Swindon & Cricklade Railway, particularly the replacement of steel girders over the river Ray at Blunsdon. Here also the station had been completely restored by August 1988. Train services are operating in the vicinity of Blunsdon and the track has been extended to a new station and engine shed at Hayes Knoll, where there is a signal box transferred from the GWR at Rowley Regis. It is planned to extend the line, away from the original trackbed, to Moulden Hill Country Park and perhaps further to Sparcells. The railway is open to the public every weekend. There are special attractions during the year from Easter to October. In December there are the Santa trains.

To work the trains there is an interesting collection of locomotives. GWR 0-6-2T no. 5637 and 4-6-0 no. 7903 *Foremarke Hall* are the principal ones, supplemented by Barclay 0-4-0ST *Richard Trevithick* (2354/1954) and diesels.

51. Talyllyn Railway

Headquarters. Wharf station, Tywyn, Gwynedd LL36 9EY. Telephone: 01654 710472.
Origin. Talyllyn Railway: opened 1866.

The Talyllyn Railway was surveyed and constructed by James Swinton Spooner. It was 6½ miles (10.2 km) in length with a gauge of 2 feet 3 inches (686 mm) and its primary purpose was the conveyance of slate from the mountain quarry to the sea. There is a steadily rising gradient from Tywyn to Abergynolwyn, and the company was part of the larger Abergynolwyn Slate and Slab Company Ltd, which had purchased the quarry at Bryn Eglwys. When the decline in the demand for slates began the railway lost its principal source of revenue, but there was a small but regular income from passenger traffic, and the owner of the railway since 1911, Sir Henry Haydn Jones, kept the line open. When he died in 1950 there seemed no option but to close the railway down. Fortunately several enthusiasts decided to try to revive the line, one of them being the late L. T. C. Rolt. He was not only an extremely able engineer, having served his apprenticeship with Kerr Stuart & Company, but was also a facile writer. He undertook to manage the railway for the newly formed Talyllyn Railway Preservation Society, the actual owners being a new company named Talyllyn Holdings Ltd.

Because the rolling stock, track and general equipment were almost worn out, there were great difficulties in maintaining a

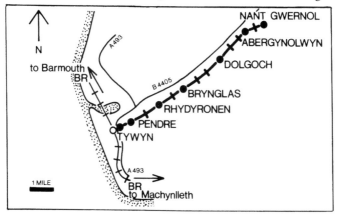

Talyllyn Railway. Locomotive no. 1 'Talyllyn' at Abergynolwyn. This is one of the original engines by Fletcher Jennings & Company of Whitehaven and dates from 1865.

regular service. Mr Rolt's unceasing efforts are recounted in his book *Railway Adventure*, which every railway enthusiast should possess. The society was formed in 1950 and therefore has the honour of being the first in the field. The success which has attended their efforts has inspired others until today there are over one hundred preserved railways, societies with rolling stock and museums. The new manager worked to such purpose that by the end of his second year in office (1952) it was obvious that the Talyllyn Railway had a future. He then left to take up work elsewhere. In 1953, when the author spent some days on the railway, he found that, despite much labour, there were places where the grass was still above rail level. His work of firing no. 4 *Edward Thomas* was not difficult as the engine steamed well, but the grass crushed by the driving wheels formed a perfect lubricant, and only the skill of the driver took the trains up to Abergynolwyn without stalling.

Since that time an enormous improvement has been effected. More locomotives and rolling stock have been acquired and the station at Tywyn Wharf has been enlarged to include refreshment rooms, a shop and a museum. The workshops at Tywyn Pendre have been re-equipped, new passing loops at stations installed, and Abergynolwyn station has been entirely reconstructed, now having a large refreshment room. But doubtless the greatest achievement has been the ³/₄ mile (1100 metre) extension from Abergynolwyn to Nant Gwernol, giving a run of 7¹/₄ miles (11 km). The stations are Tywyn Wharf, Tywyn Pendre, Rhydyronen, Brynglas, Dolgoch, Abergynolwyn, and Nant Gwernol.

There is a daily service from March to October, with the following special events: in May, the Tom Rolt Vintage Vehicle Rally; in July, Victorian Week; in August 'Race the Train', when runners compete to beat the train; and in December, Santa specials. The scenic journey along the valley includes Dolgoch viaduct.

The railway possesses the following locomotives: 0-4-2ST *Talyllyn*; 0-4-0T *Dolgoch* (these two are of the original stock); 0-4-2STs *Sir Haydn* and *Edward Thomas*; 0-4-0T *Douglas*. A new 0-4-2T locomotive has been built at Tywyn, named *Tom Rolt*. The passenger stock is made up of original Talyllyn coaches and some from the Corris and Glyn Valley railways. It is the only railway that can turn out the whole of its original stock dating from 1865-6, comprising the two original locomotives, four coaches and brake van/ticket office. The line attracts 50,000 passengers a year.

52. Tanfield Railway

Headquarters. Old Marley Hill, Sunniside, Tyne and Wear. Telephone: 0191-274 2002.
Origin. Tanfield Wagonway: opened 1725, closed 1962.

This preserved railway is unique in maintaining a train service over a track which has been in use for 270 years. Until the invention of the steam engine coal from the mine at Tanfield was moved in chaldron wagons hauled by horses. At the south end of the railway is the Causey Arch, said to be the first railway bridge ever built. Owing to the hilly nature of the countryside the earthworks are of considerable size, and the trains today run along the Causey embankment, 100 feet (30 metres) high. The railway is 3 miles (4.8 km) in length.

Since 1980 the railway has succeeded in collecting an impressive number of industrial locomotives, as follows: Hawthorne Leslie – 0-4-0ST no. 3 *Holwell* (1873), *Cyclops* (1907), no. 21 (7796/1954), *Sir Cecil A. Cochrane* (1948), 7763/1934, and 0-6-0ST *Stagshaw* (1923); Andrew Barclay – 0-6-0ST *Horden* (1906), 0-4-0ST no. 32 (1920); Hudswell Clarke – 0-4-0ST *Irwell* (1937).

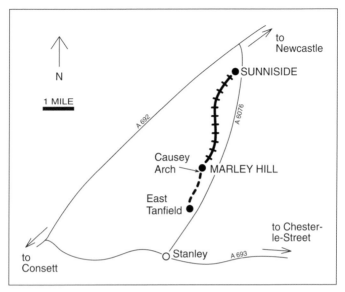

Altogether there are twenty-five steam engines and two diesels. Among the collection of coaching stock are a North Eastern Railway saloon and a Great Northern six-wheeled carriage.

The Tanfield Railway is open on every Sunday and bank holiday from January to November, and also on Wednesdays and Saturdays in July and August. Members of the public are invited to visit the railway in July and August to see 'A Workshop in Steam'. In December the usual Santa and Mince Pie Specials are run, one train having the distinctive name of 'North Pole Express'.

53. Vale of Rheidol Railway

Headquarters. Aberystwyth, Dyfed. Telephone: 01970 625819.
Origin. Vale of Rheidol Railway: opened 1902, absorbed by Cambrian Railways 1913, passed to the Great Western Railway 1924, passed to British Railways 1948. Operated by the Brecon Mountain Railway Company from 1989 to 1996, when it was sold to a charitable trust.

The original Vale of Rheidol Railway was built for the conveyance of mineral ores, freight and passengers. Constructed to the gauge of 1 foot 11½ inches (597 mm) it ran east from Aberystwyth almost on the level for the first 5 miles (8 km), approximately to Capel Bangor, and then ascended the valley for the next 7 miles (11 km) at a gradient of 1 in 50. It prospered sufficiently to attract the Cambrian Railways as buyers in 1913. It was spared the indignity, suffered by so many light railways in the First World War, of having its track lifted, and after hostilities it resumed its role, but mostly with passenger traffic. The Second World War stopped all traffic for four years, but since nationalisation in 1948 it has carried on. After a boom period stagnation crept in until in 1970 the Vale of Rheidol Railway Supporters Association was created, so that with help from volunteers and plenty of publicity the railway has thriven and today carries 60,000 passengers a year.

Trains run daily from March to October. The scenery all along the line is most impressive, and the sound of the engines will please all steam lovers. High up in the valley, on the opposite side,

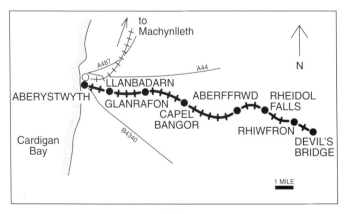

Vale of Rheidol Railway. 2-6-2T no. 7 'Owain Glyndwr' climbing to Devil's Bridge.

one can see the 'stag', which is the outline of the animal made by the waste tippings from the lead mines. The stations are Aberystwyth (with refreshment room), Llanbadarn, Glanrafon, Capel Bangor, Nantyronen, Aberffrwd, Rheidol Falls, Rhiwfron and Devil's Bridge. The last has a shop and refreshment room. A short walk from the station brings the visitor to Devil's Bridge, which consists of three bridges, one above the other, dating from different periods.

There are three locomotives, all of handsome appearance and beautifully maintained. They are all 2-6-2Ts, no. 7 *Owain Glyndwr*, no. 8 *Llywelyn* and no. 9 *Prince of Wales*, and are now oil-fired to eliminate the risk of lineside fires. The coaching stock is all of the bogie type, some coaches having open sides, while most are all enclosed. Air brakes have now been fitted instead of vacuum.

54. Wells & Walsingham Light Railway

Headquarters. Railway Station, Stiffkey Road, Wells-next-the-Sea, Norfolk. Telephone: 01328 710439.

Origin. Wells and Fakenham branch of the Eastern Counties Railway: opened 1st December 1857, closed 5th October 1964.

The opening of the Wells & Walsingham Light Railway in 1982 was the result of the expenditure of much energy to clear the trackbed of the inevitable vegetation accumulated over nearly eighteen years of neglect. The route of 4 miles (6.4 km) of 10¼ inch (260 mm) gauge is claimed to be the longest of this gauge in the world. The original standard-gauge railway had lasted for 107 years, passing from the ownership of the Eastern Counties to the Great Eastern in 1862, to the London & North Eastern in 1923 and finally to British Rail in 1948. But in this quiet part of East Anglia such a line could hardly expect to survive the Beeching era.

Wells-next-the-Sea is a most attractive town despite its having

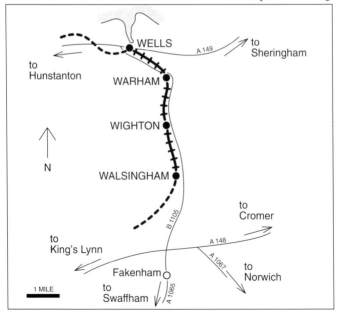

Wells & Walsingham Light Railway. Garratt 2-6-0+0-6-2 locomotive no. 3 'Norfolk Hero'.

lost most of its coastal shipping, and Walsingham is well-known for its two shrines. Visitors will find not only a very interesting railway but a countryside which abounds in ancient churches, castles and camps. Moreover, the railway not only caters for visitors but, by opening two halts, Warham St Mary and Wighton, provides a service for local shoppers. East Anglia is not a flat countryside and those who travel on the railway will find that sometimes they are on a very high embankment and at other times in deep cuttings. At the south end of the line the gradient up to Walsingham through Barnards Cutting is 1 in 29.

Between 1982 and 1985 the trains were hauled by 0-6-0T *Pilgrim* but in the meantime a fascinating locomotive was being manufactured at the works of Neil Simkins at Ashby de la Zouch. This is a Garratt with wheel arrangement 2-6-0+0-6-2, weighing 3 tons in working order. The four cylinders are of 4 inch (101 mm) bore by 5½ inch (140 mm) stroke, with a boiler providing superheated steam at 140 pounds per square inch. This large engine bears the name *Norfolk Hero* and entered service in 1986, since when it has had no difficulty with the heaviest trains. An Alan Keef 0-6-0 petrol locomotive *Weasel* is used for winter work and as back-up. The coaching stock, all of the bogie type, was originally open, but now the carriages have roofs and the large windows provide good views of the country.

Trains run every day from Easter until the end of September, and also for Norfolk schools' half-term week. There are five trains each way from May to mid September.

The railway owes its prosperity to the capable management of Commander Roy W. Francis RN (retired), to whom I am indebted for the above details. There is a Wells & Walsingham Railway Support Group under the patronage of Viscount Coke.

55. Welsh Highland Railway

Headquarters. Gelerts Farm, Madoc Street West, Porthmadog, Gwynedd; telephone: 01766 513402. Harbour station, Porthmadog, Gwynedd; telephone 01766 512340.

Origin. North Wales Narrow Gauge Railway: opened 15th August 1877, closed 1937.

After the North Wales Narrow Gauge Railway had been operating for twenty-four years it was joined by another line with the same gauge (1 foot 11^1/$_2$ inches, 597 mm). This was the Porthmadog, Beddgelert & South Snowdon Railway and they amalgamated in 1922 by virtue of the Welsh Highland Light Railway Order. This railway ran for 22 miles (35 km) through beautiful scenery from Dinas (near Caernarfon), through Rhyd Ddu, Beddgelert and the Aberglaslyn Pass. Next it passed through a tunnel 300 yards (274 metres) in length on to the high Nantmor embankment, and so to Porthmadog. The long trade depression after 1929 and the growth in the use of the private car caused the railway to become unprofitable and it was closed in 1937. Unfortunately the whole of the railway was sold by auction – locomotives, rolling stock, plant and track.

Thus for nearly a quarter of a century only the trackbed remained, but in 1961 a group of enthusiasts was determined to revive the railway and in 1964 they formed the Welsh Highland Light Railway (1964) Ltd. The new railway enjoyed the co-operation of the Gwynedd County Council and in 1973 they were able to purchase the British Rail siding at Porthmadog. A mile (1.6 km) of track was laid in 1980 and a Light Railway Order was obtained, since when train services have operated. At present Pen-y-Mount is the terminus. Train services are provided from May to October and the ticket includes a conducted tour of items of historic interest and the current works in hand.

The locomotive stock at present includes the famous *Russell*, a

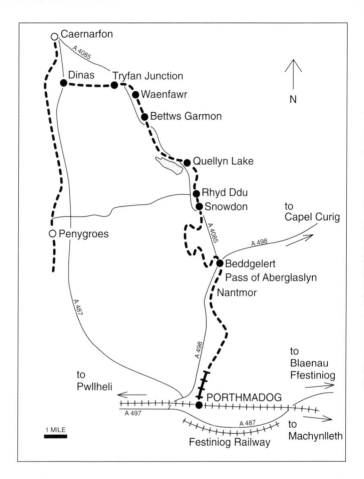

2-6-2T locomotive built by Hunslet in 1906, and therefore a survivor from the original stock. It has been restored to full working order. Other locomotives are Peckett 0-4-2T *Karen* (2024/1942), Bagnall 0-4-2Ts *Gelert* (3050/1953) and *Moel Tryfan* (3023/1953), 4-4-0T *Sinembe*, also from Bagnall (2287/1926), and former South African Railways class NG15 2-8-2 no. 120. Another engine is named *Pedemoura*, a 0-6-0T from the works of Orenstein & Koppel (10808/1924). There are nine diesel engines.

The ambition of the Welsh Highland Railway (1964) Ltd was naturally to reopen the former railway in its entirety, but in this project they had competitors – the Festiniog Railway. A new

Welsh Highland Railway. Bagnall 0-4-2T 'Gelert' with a train near Porthmadog.

Light Railway Order was necessary, and despite the strong claim by the Welsh Highland Railway (1964) Ltd, the Department of Transport, on 20th July 1994, awarded the LRO to the Festiniog Railway. The ultimate aim is to reopen the whole of the original Welsh Highland Railway from Porthmadog to Dinas and in passing through such delightful scenery a light railway abounds in sharp curves and steep gradients. This is particularly the case between Beddgelert and Rhyd Ddu. Accordingly orders have been placed with the South African Railways for five of their powerful NGG class Garratt locomotives, which are now surplus to requirements. These engines are of the 2-6-2+2-6-2 wheel arrangement, were built by Hunslet Taylor in 1968 and are expected to arrive in Wales in 1996. When ultimately the whole 22 miles (35 km) of the Welsh Highland Railway are reopened Wales will have one of the most beautiful lines in Britain.

56. Welshpool & Llanfair Light Railway

Headquarters. Llanfair Caereinion, Powys. Telephone: 01938 810441.
Origin. Welshpool & Llanfair Light Railway Company: opened 1903, closed to passengers 1931 and to freight 1956.

Wales has a double attraction for holidaymakers. There is the scenery, but also no fewer than ten railways in working order, nearly always by steam, and the number is growing. As the coastal districts are well served, the Welshpool & Llanfair Railway fills in the gap in central Wales. The original light railway served a useful purpose until motorcars drew away the passengers but the freight traffic was maintained for twenty-five years after the last passenger train had run. The Cambrian Railways supplied locomotives and stock from the inception and maintained full services. It was the Great Western which withdrew the passenger trains and this was obviously due to the national depression of trade, as the GWR had for years endeavoured to stimulate its passenger receipts by opening halts all over its system. A study of Bradshaw from, say, 1904 to 1934 reveals the enterprise of the GWR in this respect.

In 1960, four years after the final closure, the Welshpool & Llanfair Light Railway Preservation Company Ltd was formed. This is yet another instance of enthusiasm and perseverance triumphing over difficulties. For example, the important section of the line running through the town of Welshpool had to be abandoned as permission was refused on the grounds that vehicular traffic conflicted with the operation of trains. Then, soon after the

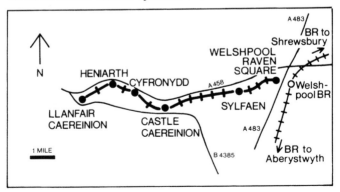

130

Welshpool & Llanfair Light Railway. 0-6-0T no. 1 'The Earl' on its way to Llanfair with a train of Zillerthalbahn coaches.

first train had run in 1963, severe weather caused flooding and the bridge over the river Banwy was damaged. This meant that the run of 5$^{1}/_{2}$ miles (9 km) along the 2 foot 6 inch (762 mm) gauge track had to be cut back to 1$^{1}/_{2}$ miles (2 km) until repairs had been carried out. From 1965 the normal train service was restored between Llanfair and Sylfaen. The railway has now reached Raven Square, Welshpool.

There is a train service at every weekend from April to October, then on Tuesdays, Wednesdays and Thursdays during June and July, and daily in August and September. The journey is very pretty, being for the first 2 miles (3.2 km) along the banks of the river Banwy. If the district is less mountainous than in the north, there are nevertheless severe gradients with stretches of 1 in 33 and 1 in 29. The railway attracts 45,000 visitors a year. The stations are Llanfair Caereinion, where there are a shop, refreshment room and locomotive repair shops, Heniarth, Cyfronydd, Castle Caereinion, Sylfaen and Welshpool, Raven Square.

The railway is famous for its locomotives. There are *The Earl* and *The Countess*, both 0-6-0Ts, which are the original engines, from Beyer Peacock & Company. A small giant is the 0-8-0T *Sir Drefaldwyn*, which is Austrian-built. Then there is an 0-6-2T from Antigua, built by Kerr Stuart & Company (4404/1927), and a 2-6-2T from the Sierra Leone Government Railway (Hunslet 3815/1954). There is an assortment of bogie coaching stock, some of which comes from Sierra Leone Railways, and some quaint four-wheeled stock from the Austrian Zillerthalbahn.

57. West Somerset Railway

Headquarters. Railway Station, Minehead, Somerset. Telephone: 01643 704996; (talking timetable) 01643 707650.

Origin. West Somerset Railway: opened 1862, and the Minehead Railway, opened 1874, broad gauge; closed 1971.

The Bristol & Exeter Railway was opened throughout in 1844 and was built to a gauge of 7 feet 0$\frac{1}{4}$ inch (2140 mm). By agreement with the Great Western Railway the B&ER was to be worked by the GWR for five years, but in 1849, when the agreement was due to be renewed, the Bristol & Exeter decided to purchase their own locomotives and rolling stock. Relations between the two companies blew hot and cold for many years. Therefore, when the West Somerset and the Minehead railways were opened the Bristol & Exeter worked them. The terms for the

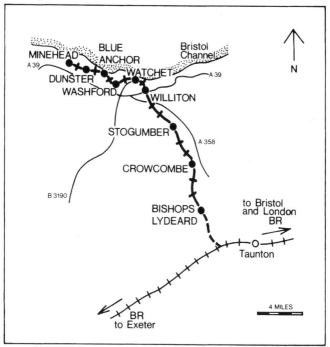

West Somerset Railway. GWR 2-6-2T no. 6106 leaving Blue Anchor on the 17.40 train from Bishop's Lydeard to Minehead on 3rd May 1993.

West Somerset (which ran for twelve years before the Minehead Railway was opened from Watchet to Minehead) were that the B&ER leased the line for 999 years and paid the WSR an annual rent of £4500 or 55 per cent of the gross receipts, whichever amount was the greater. Similar terms were arranged with the Minehead Railway, but two years later the Great Western took over and worked the lines themselves. In 1882 the branch was converted to standard gauge. The branch was used by thousands of holidaymakers in the summer months, but the winter traffic was light. The Western Region endeavoured to secure economies in 1968 by working most of the stations as unstaffed halts and running 'pay trains', whereby the guard collected fares on the move. Despite the hopes aroused by the Transport Act of 1968 that there would be fewer closures, the usual notices were posted for closure and this took place in 1971.

There was sufficient keenness in the locality for the formation of the West Somerset Railway Association in 1971 with headquarters at Bishop's Lydeard, to be followed by the West Somerset Railway Company in the same year with their centre at Minehead. This was necessary in order to obtain a Light Railway Order, which arrived

West Somerset Railway. Somerset & Dorset Joint Railway 2-8-0 no. 88 on a train near Stogumber.

via British Rail in 1975. The branch was then reopened in stages, first Minehead to Dunster, 3 miles (4.8 km), in 1976, and so gradually towards Norton Fitzwarren and Taunton. The West Somerset has now reached Bishop's Lydeard, which is likely to remain the terminus. The present length is 19^1/$_2$ miles (31.2 km).

Trains run in March at weekends, and in April daily except Mondays and Tuesdays. In May certain Tuesdays are excepted, but full daily services are maintained from June to September inclusive. In the final month of operation, October, some Thursdays are without trains.

At Bishop's Lydeard in April there is a Model Railway Weekend, in May a Spring Gala Weeekend, and in August a Vintage Rally. In September there is a special steam weekend, followed by Friends of Thomas the Tank Engine in October. In this month also there is a special diesel weekend.

The stations are Minehead, with refreshment room and shop, Dunster, Blue Anchor, Washford, Watchet, Doniford Beach halt, Williton, Stogumber, Crowcombe and Bishop's Lydeard.

In the days of BR steam working the branch was a haunt of pannier tanks and Moguls, and nos. 3736 and 6360 seemed to have a liking for the jaunt to Minehead, as they were often seen. The later days saw the normal diesel multiple-unit sets. Today the Great Western flavour has been well maintained with GWR 0-6–0PT no. 6412 and 2-6-2Ts nos. 4561 and 5542, as well as WR 4-6-0 no. 7820 *Dinmore Manor*, 2-8-0 no. 3850 and 2-6-2T no. 4160.

An industrial engine, the Bagnall 0-6-0ST *Victor*, is excellent as a standby. A Ruston & Hornsby diesel engine makes a useful shunter, and there are two ex-BR diesel multiple-unit sets. The Somerset & Dorset Joint Railway Museum Trust owns a 2-8-0 (no. 53808) which formerly ran on the S&DJR, and all those who loved the Somerset & Dorset are delighted that the engine is now in working order. The Diesel and Electric Group owns a Hymek locomotive no. 7017 and D1035 *Western Yeoman*.

Bishop's Lydeard and Crowcombe have churches of such outstanding beauty that they should on no account be missed.

Other interesting railways

The following is a list of railways, not necessarily preserved, which the reader may wish to visit when in the locality.

Alderney Railway, St Anne's House, Victoria Street, Alderney, Channel Islands. Standard gauge. Length 2 miles.

Alford Valley Railway, Aberdeen. Telephone: 01336 2052. Gauge 2 feet. Length 1 mile.

Amerton Railway, Amerton Farm, Stowe by Chartley, Stafford. Telephone: 01889 270294 or 270328. Gauge 2 feet. Length $^3/_4$ mile.

Audley End Miniature Railway, Audley End House, Saffron Walden, Essex. Telephone: 01799 22354. Gauge $10^1/_4$ inches. Length 1 mile.

Avon Valley Railway, Bitton station, Bristol. Telephone: 01275 822727. Standard gauge. Length 3 miles.

Ayrshire Railway Preservation Group, Dalmellington, Ayrshire. Standard gauge. Length 3 miles.

Barton House Railway, Barton House, Wroxham, Norfolk. Telephone: 01605 32470. Gauge $3^1/_2$ inches. Length 80 yards.

Beer Heights Light Railway, Beer, Devon. Telephone: 01297 21542. Gauge $7^1/_4$ inches. Length $1^1/_2$ miles.

Bicton Woodland Railway, Bicton Park, East Budleigh, Devon. Telephone: 01395 68465. Gauge 18 inches. Length $1^1/_4$ miles.

Blenheim Palace Miniature Railway, Blenheim Palace, Woodstock, Oxfordshire. Telephone: 01993 811805. Gauge 15 inches. Length $^1/_2$ mile.

Bowes Railway, Springwell, Gateshead, Tyne and Wear. Telephone: 0191-416 1847. Standard gauge. Length $^1/_4$ mile.

Brechin Railway, Brechin, Angus. Telephone: 01356 622992. Standard gauge. Length 4 miles.

Bristol Docks Railway, City Docks, Bristol, Avon. Telephone: 01272 251470. Standard gauge. Length $^1/_2$ mile.

Buckinghamshire Railway Centre, Quainton Road station, Quainton, Aylesbury, Buckinghamshire. Telephone: 01296 655720; (recorded message) 01296 655450. Standard gauge.

Cadeby Light Railway, Cadeby Rectory, Market Bosworth, Leicestershire. Telephone: 01455 290462. Length 400 yards.

Cambrian Railways Society, Oswestry, Shropshire. Telephone: 01691 661648. Standard gauge.

Cleethorpes Coast Light Railway, King's Road, Cleethorpes, South Humberside. Telephone: 01472 602118. Gauge 15 inches. Length 1 mile.

Dobwalls Theme Park, Dobwalls, Liskeard, Cornwall. Telephone: 01579 20325. Gauge 7¼ inches.

Drusillas Park Railway, Alfriston, East Sussex. Gauge 2 feet.

East Anglian Railway Museum, Chappel & Wakes Colne station, Colchester, Essex. Telephone: 01787 52571. Standard gauge. Length ½ mile.

East Kent Light Railway, Shepherdswell station, Dover, Kent. Standard gauge. Length 4 miles.

Echills Wood Railway, Echills Wood, Stoneleigh, Warwickshire. Telephone: 01203 555100. Gauge 7¼ inches. Length ½ mile.

Exmouth Miniature Railway, Exmouth, Devon.

Fakenham & Dereham Railway Society, Hardingham, Norfolk. Standard gauge.

Great Cockrow Railway, Lyne, Chertsey, Surrey. Gauge 7¼ inches. Length 1 mile.

Great Orme Railway, Victoria station, Llandudno, Gwynedd. Telephone: 01492 870870. Gauge 3 feet 6 inches. Length 1¼ miles.

Great Western Society, Didcot station, Didcot, Oxfordshire. Telephone: 01235 817200. Standard gauge. Length ½ mile.

Haigh Hall Country Park Railway, Wigan, Lancashire. Gauge 15 inches. Length 1½ miles.

Hastings Miniature Railway, The Marina, Hastings, East Sussex. Telephone: 01424 424242. Gauge 10¼ inches. Length 1 mile.

Hollycombe Woodland Railway, Liphook, Hampshire. Telephone: 01428 723233. Gauge 2 feet. Length ½ mile.

Kerr's Miniature Railway, Arbroath, Angus. Telephone: 01241 79249. Gauge 10¼ inches.

Kessingland Miniature Railway, Suffolk Wild Life Park, Kessingland, Suffolk. Telephone: 01502 741813. Gauge 10¼ inches. Length 1¼ miles.

Kirklees Light Railway, Clayton West, Barnsley, South Yorkshire. Gauge 15 inches. Length 4 miles.

Lake Shore Railway, Boating Lake Park, South Shields, Tyne and Wear. Gauge 9½ inches. Length ⅜ mile.

Lappa Valley Railway, St Newlyn East, Cornwall. Telephone: 01872 510317. Gauge 15 inches. Length 1 mile.

Launceston Steam Railway, Launceston station, Launceston, Cornwall. Telephone: 01566 775665. Gauge 2 feet. Length 1½ miles.

The Lavender Line, Isfield station, Lewes, East Sussex. Telephone: 01825 750515. Standard gauge. Length ½ mile.

Leadhills & Wanlockhead Railway, Abington, Lanarkshire. Gauge 2 feet (610 mm). Length 2 miles (3 km).

Lightwater Valley Miniature Railway, North Stainley, Ripon, North Yorkshire. Telephone: 01765 85321. Gauge 15 inches. Length 1 mile.

Littlehampton Miniature Railway, Mewsbrook Park, Littlehampton, West Sussex. Telephone: 01906 45693. Gauge 12¼ inches. Length ½ mile.

Llechwedd Slate Caverns (Ceudwll Llechwedd), Blaenau Ffestiniog, Gwynedd. Telephone: 01766 830306. Gauge 2 feet. Length ½ mile.

Longleat Light Railway, Longleat Park, Warminster, Wiltshire. Telephone: 01985 3579. Gauge 15 inches. Length 1 mile.

Lowthers Light Railway, Wanlockhead, Elvanfoot, Lanarkshire. Gauge 2 feet.

Mangapps Farm Railway, Southminster Road, Burnham-on-Crouch, Essex. Telephone: 01621 784898. Standard gauge. Length ½ mile.

Mull & West Highland Narrow Gauge Railway Company Ltd, Craignure, Isle of Mull, Scotland. Telephone: 01680 2494. Gauge 10¼ inches. Length 2 miles.

National Tramway Museum, Cliff Quarry, Crich, Derbyshire. Telephone: 01773 852565. Standard gauge. Length 1 mile.

Newby Hall Railway, Newby Hall, Skelton-on-Ure, Ripon, North Yorkshire. Telephone: 01901 22583. Gauge 10¼ inches. Length ½ mile.

Northampton & Lamport Railway, Pitsford, Northamptonshire. Telephone: 01604 820327. Standard gauge. Length 1 mile.

Northamptonshire Ironstone Railway Trust, Hunsbury Hill, Northampton. Telephone: 01604 811130. Length 2 miles.

North Tyneside Steam Railway, Percy Main, Newcastle upon Tyne, Tyne and Wear. Standard gauge. Length 1¾ miles (2.8 km).

Nottingham Heritage Museum, Ruddington, Nottingham. Standard gauge. Length 2¾ miles.

Overstone Solarium Light Railway, Overstone Park, Sywell, Northamptonshire. Telephone: 01604 45255. Gauge 1 foot 11½ inches. Length 1 mile.

Paultons Park Railway, Ower, Romsey, Hampshire. Telephone: 01703 814442. Gauge 15 inches.

Peak Rail plc, Matlock, Derbyshire. Telephone: 01298 79898. Standard gauge. Length 5 miles.

Pembrey Country Park Railway, Llanelli, Dyfed. Telephone: 01554 63913. Gauge 2 feet. Length 1 mile.

Pleasurewood Hills Railway, Corton Road, Gunton, Lowestoft, Suffolk. Telephone: 01502 513626. Gauge 7¼ inches. Length 2 miles.

Pontypool & Blaenafon Railway Society, Blaenafon, Gwent. Standard gauge.

Poole Park Miniature Railway, Poole, Dorset. Telephone: 01202 745296. Gauge 10¼ inches. Length 1 mile.

Port Errol Railway, 12 Station Place, Cruden Bay, Aberdeen. Telephone: 01779 812410. Gauge 7^1/4 inches. Length ^{1}/2 mile.

Rhyl Miniature Railway, Marine Park, Rhyl, Clwyd. Telephone: 01745 55068. Gauge 15 inches. Length 1 mile.

Rode Woodland Railway, Bath, Avon. Gauge 7^1/4 inches. Length 1 mile.

Rother Valley Railway, Killamarsh, Sheffield. Telephone: 01742 445012 or 470901. Standard gauge. Length ^{1}/2 mile.

Rudyard Lake Railway, Rudyard, Leek, Staffordshire. Telephone: 01260 272862. Gauge 10^1/2 inches. Length ^{3}/4 mile.

Ruislip Lido Railway, Ruislip, Middlesex. Telephone: 01895 633831. Gauge 15 inches. Length 1 mile.

Rutland Railway Museum, Cottesmore, Oakham, Rutland. Standard gauge.

Rydon Park Railway, Holsworthy, Devon. Gauge 10^1/4 inches.

Seaton & District Electric Tramway, Seaton, Devon. Telephone: 01297 21702. Gauge 2 feet 9 inches. Length 2^1/2 miles.

Shipley Glen Tramway, Shipley Glen, Baildon, West Yorkshire. Telephone: 01904 589010. Gauge 1 foot 8 inches. Length ^{1}/2 mile.

Southend-on-Sea Pier Railway, Southend-on-Sea, Essex. Telephone: 01702 619645. Gauge 3 feet. Length 1^1/2 miles.

Southport Pier Railway, Southport, Merseyside. Telephone: 01704 33133. Gauge 2 feet. Length ^{1}/2 mile.

Steamtown Railway Centre, Warton Road, Carnforth, Lancashire. Telephone: 01524 732100. Standard gauge.

Steeple Grange Light Railway, Wirksworth, Derbyshire. Gauge 18 inches. Length 200 yards.

Strathaven Miniature Railway, George Allan Park, East Kilbride, Lanarkshire. Telephone: 01355 228777. Gauge 7^1/4 inches. Length ^{1}/4 mile.

Summerlee Heritage Park, Coatbridge, Lanarkshire. Telephone: 01236 22085. Standard gauge. Length ^{1}/2 mile.

Swansea Vale Railway, 17 Orpheus Road, Ynysforgan, Swansea, West Glamorgan. Standard gauge.

Teifi Valley Railway, Henllan station, Llandysul, Dyfed. Telephone: 01559 371077. Gauge 2 feet. Length 1 mile.

Telford & Horsehay Steam Trust, Telford, Shropshire. Telephone: 01952 503880. Standard gauge. Length 1^1/2 miles.

Thoresby Hall Miniature Railway, Thoresby Park, Ollerton, Nottinghamshire. Gauge 10^1/4 inches. Length ^{1}/2 mile.

Trago Mills Miniature Railway, Newton Abbot, Devon. Telephone: 01579 20584. Gauge 10^1/4 inches. Length 1 mile.

Vanstone Woodland Railway, Vanstone Park Garden Centre, Codicote, Hertfordshire. Telephone: 01438 820412. Gauge

$10^1/_4$ inches. Length $^1/_2$ mile.

Volk's Electric Railway, 285 Madeira Drive, Brighton, East Sussex BN2 1EN. Telephone: 01273 681086. Gauge 2 feet $8^1/_2$ inches. Length $1^1/_4$ miles.

Wells Harbour Railway, Wells-next-the-Sea, Norfolk. Gauge $10^1/_4$ inches. Length 1 mile.

West Lancashire Light Railway, Hesketh Bank, Southport, Merseyside. Telephone: 01942 218078. Gauge 2 feet.

Whorlton Lido Railway, Whorlton Lido, Barnard Castle, County Durham. Telephone: 01833 27397. Gauge 15 inches. Length $^1/_2$ mile.

Further reading

Allen, C.J. *The Great Eastern Railway*. Ian Allan, 1956.

Allen, C.J. *North Eastern Railway*. Ian Allan, 1974.

Awdry, Rev. W. *A Guide to the Steam Railways of Great Britain*. Pelham Books, 1979.

Davies, W.J.K. *Ravenglass & Eskdale Railway*. David & Charles, 1989.

Dow, George. *Great Central*. Locomotive Publishing Company, 1960.

Ellis, C. Hamilton. *London Brighton & South Coast Railway*. Ian Allan, 1971.

Nock, O.S. *History of the Great Western Railway*, Part III. Ian Allan, 1967.

Robbins, M. *The Isle of Wight Railways*. Oakwood Press, 1963.

Rolt, L.T.C. *Railway Adventure*. David & Charles, 1971.

Warren, Alan. *Rescued from Barry*. David & Charles, 1983.

Waters, L. *Didcot Junction and Railway Centre*. Ian Allan, 1989.

Welsh, M.S. *Rails to Sheffield Park*. Kingfisher Railway Productions, 1989.

Wrottesley, A.J. *Midland & Great Northern Joint Railway*. David & Charles, 1970.

Dean Forest Railway. Hunslet 0-6-0ST 'Wilbert' at Norchard station (low level) in 1992.

Index

Page numbers in italic refer to illustrations.